BEWARE THE FULL MOON

In 1961, Inspector Wilfred Faust of the Philadelphia Police Department filed a report with the American Institute of Medical Climatology. According to Inspector Faust, "People whose antisocial behavior had psychotic roots—such as firebugs, kleptomaniacs, destructive drivers, and homicidal alcoholics—seemed to go on a rampage as the moon rounded, calming down as the moon waned."

Thomas P. Brophy, Chief of New York City's Bureau of Fire Investigation, claimed that his experience had taught him to expect more fires on nights when the moon was full than at any other time of the month. During such times, he and his men maintained their most watchful state of alert, waiting for the inevitable rash of fires they knew they would be called upon to fight.

MOON MADNESS

E. L. Abel

A FAWCETT GOLD MEDAL BOOK

Fawcett Publications, Inc., Greenwich, Connecticut

The Author and Publisher wish to thank Llewellyn Publications for permission to reprint material published in the *Moon Sign Book*.

MOON MADNESS

ISBN 0-449-13697-3

Printed in the United States of America

10 9 8 7 6 5 4 3 2 1

Contents

Moon Madness

THE WORLD of science is a never-ending whodunit in which the scientist is the detective trying to solve the mystery. Instead of sitting behind an old beat-up desk in a rundown building waiting for a seductive woman to enter his office with her problem, the Sam Spade of the scientific world usually wears a shabby white frock, and instead of sitting at his desk he is usually hunched over a microscope squinting at tiny animals swimming around on a glass slide, or watching a rat run down a maze. Both the detective and the scientist are faced with enigmas. The enigmas that the scientist may have to contend with are rarely as dramatic as solving the mystery of the murdered man discovered in a room locked from the inside, but it could be a matter of life and death all the same. Trying to find the causes and cures for cancer, a disease that kills millions of people, may not be the stuff that mystery thrillers are made of, but the mystery and the suspense are all there nonetheless.

Why does the heart beat? How does blood flow uphill against gravity? How do birds fly, and how do they know where to fly when winter comes? Why do we need sleep?

How can some people get up exactly at the same time each day without the aid of an alarm clock? Such questions could be multiplied *ad infinitum*. There is simply no end to the questions one can ask about nature's mysteries.

How does the scientist go about cracking nature's mysteries? Like the police detective, he has clues which he must run down. It takes a lot of questioning, a lot of blind alleys, frustrations, problems that have to be solved before further progress can be made, checking and rechecking of facts that are already known, until finally he is able, if he is lucky, to isolate the one something that is responsible for a particular happening.

If it is a disease he is studying, that one something may be a virus or a bacterium of some sort. Having identified a likely culprit, the suspect must then be given a fair and impartial trial. It must be subjected to exhaustive tests which will certainly be challenged by a jury of the scientist's colleagues. When finally there is no doubt that the guilty culprit has been caught, the next step is to try to put it out of commission. If he is lucky, the scientist can come up with a vaccine to kill the life-robbing virus, and in so doing, he may be able to put an end to the suffering caused by this invading organism. Smallpox and polio are only two such diseases which have almost been eradicated on this continent as a result of vaccines which scientists have given us as a result of their detective work.

Not all scientists work with diseases, however, and often their problems are of a very different nature and require very different special techniques. For example, how does one study the effects of too much sunlight on the human body? We cannot subject people to the sun for long periods merely to study what will happen. Instead, if we want to know the answers to such questions, we have to make guesses from experiments with animals or we have to keep under close scrutiny people who have accidently been exposed to too much sunlight. This is often the way we learn about the hazards of some particular agent. An animal, for example, will be exposed to a great deal of ultraviolet radiation, the kind of radiation that comes from the sun and causes us to sunburn. The animal chosen is usually a mammal. We too are mammals. Maybe the animal can warn us about the dangers of absorbing too much radiation. Maybe it can also inform us, by serving as an experimental subject, of the best way of treating cases of overexposure to such sources of radiation. If the method works, and we are sure that it poses no dangers itself, then it can be tried on people.

Working with ultraviolet rays is a way scientists have of studying the effects of too much sunlight on the body. But imagine the difficulties of conducting such research using direct sunlight. There could be no work on cloudy days, and one could really conduct such research only in the summer. Nights would be a complete waste. Since there is no way of influencing the sun, research of this type would be very time-consuming and difficult. Fortunately, however, scientists know that it is the ultraviolet rays of the sun that cause sunburn and they are able to produce ultraviolet light in their laboratories.

The scientist who wants to study how the moon affects living organisms on earth is faced with a particularly difficult problem. Unlike his colleagues in other areas of science, he cannot manipulate the thing he wishes to study. Instead, he must wait patiently for the moon to make its natural revolution around the earth. For the scientist who is interested in lunar effects, patience is not a virtue, it is a necessity. If he wants to see how the full moon affects living things, be they plant, animal, or human, he must make his observations at roughly monthly intervals. If he wants to recheck his findings, he has to wait another month. No wonder, then, that so few scientists are willing to devote their lives to the study of lunar effects on living organisms.

At first, it was only our predominantly agrarian an
cestors who were willing or who actually had the tim
and patience to inquire into the lunar mystery. Month
after month, year after year, they watched the change
in plant growth, the changes in their animals, and the
changes in their neighbors. After centuries of such obser
vations, it eventually became clear to these people tha
during certain phases of the moon, seeds would germi
nate faster, plants would grow taller, animals would
become restless, and their neighbors would sometime
act very peculiarly.

For a long time, these observations were treated a
folklore or superstition by the scientific world. The greates
obstacle to the acknowledgment of a lunar effect on earth'
inhabitants was the enormous difficulty in explaining how
such an influence could be transmitted across the thou
sands of miles separating the moon from the earth. Ou
ancestors implicitly believed that the moon exerted cer
tain powers over the earth simply because they observed
that the repetition of many events coincided with luna
cycles. The growth of the scientific spirit, however, made
men cautious in attributing such events to the influence
of the moon. In this respect, scientific sophistication
actually retarded our understanding of the cosmic con
nection between the moon and the earth. Since many
scientists are unhappy unless they can account for events
in nature in terms of rational and general principles, they
have found it more comforting to deny what they do no
understand than to admit something exists but is as ye
unexplainable. Fortunately, not all scientists dismiss every
thing they do not understand as unimportant or as super
stition. Several well-respected men of science have in fac
recently rediscovered many of the long-known relation
ships between the movements of the moon and life or
earth. Their studies leave no doubt that the moon does
affect our daily lives in many direct and indirect ways.

In this book, I have attempted to bring together this

information, from several different areas of science, which illustrates some of these more amazing and important influences. In doing so, I have tried to reduce the technical language as much as possible. This should enable the reader to gain a clearer and wider appreciation of the facts and help him understand what is already known and what is still to be discovered about the subject.

In writing any book, there are always countless people to thank for their help and cooperation. Two individuals that warrant special acknowledgment in this regard are my wife, Barbara Buckley, and my friend and colleague, Dr. James York. Both of them read the manuscript thoroughly and offered valuable criticisms.

1. Time, Blood, and the Moon

FROM the beginnings of recorded history, the belief has existed that the moon exerts a definite and precise influence over growth and decay, fertility and infertility, disease and health, and even the destinies of nations.

Those acquainted with Greek history will remember that in 490 B.C. the Persian army threatened to overrun Greece and was only prevented from doing so by the valiant and solitary stand of the Athenians at the Battle of Marathon. The reason the Athenians had to fight alone, without the help of their powerful Spartan allies, was that it was a rule of the Spartans never to begin a war unless the moon was full. This belief kept them from marching to the aid of the outnumbered Athenians. As a result, the Spartans remained in their camps while the defense of Greece was left to the Athenians. Had the Athenians entertained the same rule of military conduct, or had they fought less gloriously, it is possible that the entire course of Western civilization might have been completely different.

Indeed, the movements of the moon were considered to be of profound importance by nearly all the nations of the ancient world. The moon was once worshiped as a god, superior even to the god of the sun. The Hebrews of the Old Testament, for example, held the moon in particular veneration. The time of the new moon, which signaled the beginning of the month for them, was celebrated with pomp and ceremony as an important religious event. On such days the people were obliged to lay down their tools and put aside their daily activities so that they could better observe these rites. The reason for this festivity was the belief that the moon influenced the growth of vegetation and that the fertility of crops was ensured if they were sown when the moon itself was growing. Hence, the appearance of the new moon was the signal that crop growth was about to take place.

But the veneration of the moon was not due solely to its influence on the growth of plants; the moon was believed to influence many other important events as well. For one thing, the fact that the time between new moons coincided almost exactly with the duration of the menstrual cycle in women suggested that this heavenly body was somehow connected with human fertility. Among the Babylonians, it was believed that Ishtar, the Moon Goddess, had her monthly bleeding at the time of the full moon. Accordingly, this period was called the evil day or "Sabattu," from whence we get our own word "sabbath."

In addition to its position of importance as a deity whose waxing and waning movements seemed to be the heavenly representation of generation and regeneration, birth and death, and growth and decay, the moon also provided man with a means of reckoning time in units longer than the night-and-day cycle of the sun. Indeed, the first calendars ever devised were based upon the all-important lunar cycle, and these calendars continued to be used for thousands of years until more precise methods of reckoning time were invented.

Owing to the alleged influence of the moon on the

humors of the body, the medical profession has from early times paid close attention to the movements of the moon. As late as the eighteenth century, many physicians still adhered to the Hippocratic doctrine (fifth century B.C.) that the body contains four basic humors—blood, phlegm, yellow bile, and black bile. These humors, it was believed, accounted for the four basic temperaments—the sanguine, the phlegmatic, the choleric, and the melancholic. In addition, these four humors were subdivided into hot and cold and dry and moist. In the same way that the moon was observed to control the rise and fall of the tides in the sea, it was likewise believed to affect the movements of these humors in the body. When the influence was such that it produced an imbalance in some people, the afflicted individuals were said to be "out of humor" and therefore ill. A remnant of this belief is also apparent in terms like "cold-blooded," "cold-hearted," "hot-blooded," and "hot-tempered."

A direct consequence of this belief in the role of the humors in disease and temperament was the standard practice among physicians of drawing blood from those who were sick in any way. The English physician Gilbertus Anglicus (1170–1230 A.D.) tells us of a case in which a woman came to him complaining of an excruciating pain in her right wrist. Since she was a rather corpulent woman, Gilbert felt that her problem was that she was too full-blooded, and he immediately set out to correct that condition by cutting her right hand and left foot until she lost about a pint of blood. One hour later he removed another pint from his patient. Apparently the treatment worked, for the woman said that she wasn't in pain anymore and asked Gilbert to take more blood still so that the pain wouldn't come back.

According to one testimonial of the Middle Ages on the efficacy of this method of treatment:

Of bleeding many profits grow, and great
The spirits and the senses are renewed thereby,
Tho these men slowly by strength of mate
But these by wine restored are bye and bye;
By bleeding to the marrow cometh health.
It maketh clene your brane, releeves your eie,
It mendeth appetite, restoreth sleepe,
Correcting humors, that do waking keepe
All inward parts, and senses also clearing
It mends the voice, the smell, the hearing.

Bloodletting eventually became such a common method of treatment for pain and illness that bleeding parlors began to open up all over Europe. The red-and-white barber pole is a symbol carried over from that early time when barbers would not only trim your hair but would also cut your arms and legs for a nominal fee. The blood-stained bandages would then be hung out in front of the shop to dry like any other piece of dirty laundry. When barbers were eventually forced by law to confine their surgery to hair, they chose to retain the red-and-white symbol of their bloodletting past because it had become so indelibly associated with the profession of barbering.

With the ever increasing popularity of phlebotomy, as bloodletting was called, the art of bleeding the sick patient became an important subject that had to be mastered by all aspiring physicians. And as an integral part of his coursework in the subject, every student was counseled and exhorted by his teachers to acquaint himself with the movements of the moon if he ever hoped to be a competent practitioner of this medical art. La Martinière, a French physician of the late Middle Ages, advised his students as follows concerning the period of the moon in which to bleed a patient: "In its first quadrant [the moon] is warm and damp, at which time it is good to let the blood of sanguine persons; in its second it is warm and dry, at which time it is good to bleed the choleric; in its third quadrant it is cold and moist, and phlegmatic people

may be bled; and in its fourth it is cold and dry, at which
time it is well to bleed the melancholic."

Although bloodletting as a method of therapy is of
course no longer practiced by barbers or physicians, the
influence of the moon on the bleeding of wounds has
become a topic of current interest to physicians. Dr. Edson
J. Andrews, a surgeon in Tallahassee, Florida, has recently reported the results of a study he conducted in
which he found evidence to corroborate the ancient medical "superstition" that the amount of bleeding that occurs
during an operation and afterward is greater during the
full moon than if the surgery were done at some other
time of the month.

"It has often occurred to me, as it has to many others
performing eye, ear, nose, and throat surgery," writes
Dr. Andrews, "that at certain times the human body has
a greater predilection to excessive bleeding than at others.
There are days in the operating room when hemorrhage
is of no import; at other times, persistent and annoying
bleeding is the rule of the day."

Dr. Andrews' attention was first drawn to the influence
of the moon in this regard by his nurse, who, unbeknownst
to him, had been keeping a record of cases involving
excessive bleeding on a calendar, and with this evidence
in hand, she was able to demonstrate that these difficult
cases had indeed coincided with the period of the full
moon. His interest piqued, Dr. Andrews began a search
of the voluminous medical literature to see if any other
doctors had reported a similar observation, but nowhere
could he find any research that had been done to prove
or disprove the relationship between the moon and bleeding. "The scientists all agreed that it was folklore and
superstition and that there was no scientific basis for such
an hypothesis," he relates, "but unfortunately they had
never bothered to collect any data to substantiate their
claim." So to prove the matter one way or another, he
began to keep records of all his tonsillectomy cases

during the years 1956 through 1958.

At the conclusion of this three-year study involving over a thousand patients, Dr. Andrew found that 82 percent of all cases of excessive operative bleeding occurred between the first and third quarters of the moon, with the peak number of cases occurring around the time of the full moon. "These data have been so conclusive and convincing to me," writes Dr. Andrews, "that I threaten to become a witch doctor and operate on dark nights only, saving the moonlit nights for romance."

What Dr. Andrews had found, or rather had rediscovered, was that the influence of the moon should be recognized in treating the sick, and that failure to do so could have dire consequences for the patient. But while Dr. Andrews had to be convinced of the truth of this age-old fact, apparently many of his patients had learned of it and accepted it long before, since a large number of them put off treatment during the full moon when bleeding was at its greatest. In addressing his fellow surgeons concerning this fact, Dr. Andrews candidly admitted that "perhaps laymen know more about this than we do and are reluctant to enter the hospital at this time."

In the Department of Biology at Wichita State University, Wichita, Kansas, Professor Harry D. Rounds has been conducting experiments that prove that human blood, as well as the blood of animals and insects, contains a "life" factor with the ability to affect heart rate. It is with incredible astonishment that Professor Rounds has also discovered that the presence of this "life" factor varies in quantity according to the phase of the moon!

To demonstrate this amazing relationship between the moon and this "life" factor, Dr. Rounds took blood from a number of men after they had run up and down a few flights of stairs. The blood of mice and cockroaches was similarly taken after they had been "stressed" by shaking them in a jar or terrarium. Blood samples were taken in this manner over a period of months.

The presence of the "life" factor was determined by placing a single drop of blood on the heart of a cockroach that had been removed from the insect's body and kept "alive" in a special apparatus.

When placed on the cockroach heart, Rounds found that the blood from the stressed humans did not accelerate the beating very much, except when blood was taken shortly after the new and full moons. A similar relationship between heartbeat acceleration and blood was found when specimens from mice and cockroaches were tested. Typically, the ability of the blood from humans, mice, and cockroaches to increase heart rate dropped to zero after a period of stress, at all other times of the month.

Dr. Rounds states that the disappearance of the "life" force from the blood after a period of stress could be due to a loss of this as yet undetermined factor, a result of its being altered to the point of losing its activity. The fact that this activity is still present shortly after the new and full moons is thus singularly important, for it shows that at these times the "life force" in the body is at its highest.

These results, concludes Rounds, "leave little alternative to the hypothesis that there is some sort of a direct or indirect relationship between lunar movements and the blood chemistry of cockroaches, mice and men."

Like every other kind of discipline, science thrives as a result of continuous searching, probing, and examination of current truths. It grows in depth and breadth from generation to generation, from country to country, through the work of men who are not satisfied with the explanations of their day and who challenge cherished beliefs with better answers. If scientists are reluctant even to entertain the existence of certain possibilities, scientific progress in understanding man's relationship with his environment will come to a standstill.

The inability to explain how the moon influences events on earth seems to be the major obstacle preventing

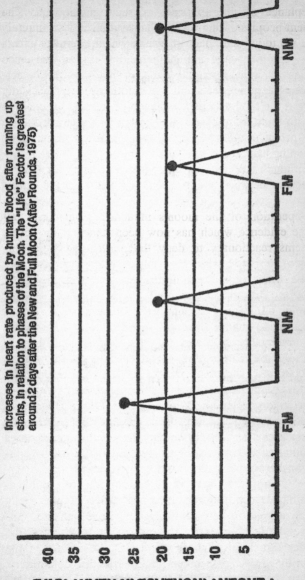

Increases in heart rate produced by human blood after running up stairs, in relation to phases of the Moon. The "Life" Factor is greatest around 2 days after the New and Full Moon (After Rounds, 1975)

PERCENT INCREASE IN HEART RATE

CYCLE OF THE MOON

acceptance of the existence of such phenomena. The ancient peoples of the world, who scrutinized less minutely than we today the chain of events which connects effects with remote causes, implicitly believed in the existence of this relationship simply because they saw the coincidence of certain effects and the condition of this heavenly body at the time. But as the growth of science has enabled men to trace more clearly the way in which changes arise and produce other changes, this empirical method of reasoning has ceased to be acceptable.

Although scientists have sought to account for the relationship between events in Nature with accepted principles, it has proved difficult to do so with reference to the operation of the moon's influence. Considering all of the evidence which has now been amassed, however, it seems reactionary to deny the existence of such influences simply because we cannot explain them.

The belief in a lunar influence on certain biological processes still remains a matter of amusement in most scientific circles, but the current of opinion is now slowly appearing to change direction. For example, in the London *Sunday Times* (March 15, 1963), Sir Bernard Lovell, the director of England's Jodrell Bank Observatory, stated his opinion concerning such matters as follows: "In the last few years some strange and inexplicable links appear to be emerging between lunar phase, rainfall, meteoric impact, magnetic storms and mental disturbances. It almost seems as though we are moving through a series of fantasies to a proof of the ancient belief in the connection between the moon and lunacy."

An impressive number of serious scientific publications have recently begun to appear which support many of the ancient beliefs to which Dr. Lovell alludes. Increases in the birth rate, the growth of plants, and the murder rate have all been related to the phases of the moon by respected members of the scientific community. It is to the examination of these and other "discoveries" that this present book is dedicated.

In the pages which follow, I have attempted to relate the ideas, the observations, and the learned opinions of the past with the findings of modern science with regard to the moon's influence on living organisms. Because of the controversial nature of the material, I have concluded this presentation with a detailed bibliography of all sources of reference. A quick glance through this material ought to convince even the most skeptical minds that the men whose work I am about to discuss are not crackpots or charlatans, but serious-minded scientists, and the journals in which they have presented their results are among the most reputable in the scientific domain.

THOUSANDS of years ago, in the primeval ages before the dawn of civilization, our ancestors must have looked up at the skies and wondered at the mystery of the heavens. The rising and setting of the sun, the appearance and disappearance of the ever-twinkling stars, and the constantly changing visage of the moon must all have aroused their curiosity and admiration. But it was the moon that evoked their gratitude as well, for it alone illuminated the darkness in which their enemies and predatory animals often lurked, waiting patiently and silently for the chance to destroy them. Moonlight was especially important when our Stone Age ancestors left their caves to become nomads, and began long and perilous journeys across the deserts of the ancient world to new and hitherto unoccupied lands. Because these journeys were often impossible in the day due to the intense heat of the sun, the early caravans usually moved at night, and at such times the moon was the only source of illumination in the barren desert.

The need to keep track of time was another important factor which increased man's reliance on the predictable activity of the moon. The sun could be used for marking

events from day to day and from season to season, but
the phases of the moon, because they are so striking and
so periodical, could be used to measure off time in periods
of seven, fourteen, twenty-one, or twenty-eight days, or
multiples thereof. Consequently, it became more con-
venient to speak of how many moons had passed than
of how many suns had come and gone. It was for this
reason that the early calendars in the ancient world were
nearly all based on the movements of the moon. "The
moon has been created for the counting of days," says
an old Jewish Midrash, and indeed, in nearly all the
fragmentary records of long-forgotten civilizations, we can
find some reference to the moon as the calendar of an-
tiquity. Even when agricultural societies began to emerge,
and the sun came to occupy an important place in the
life of the community, time was still reckoned by moons
and by dozens of moons, which were inaccurately called
"years."

The reliance on the moon for the safety of its light
and for its chronological significance contributed in no
small way to the appearance of moon cults which pro-
moted worship of the moon as a deity.

The earliest indication of such moon worship in the
ancient world comes from a 12,000-year-old prehistoric
painting which was found on the walls of a cave in the
countryside around Ariège, France. The painting depicts
a man clothed in animal skins, wearing horns on his
head and surrounded by various animals. Presumably
the caveman artist was attempting to portray a fertility
scene in which game was bountiful and the hunter could
easily locate his prey. The noteworthy feature of this
painting as far as ancient religion is concerned is the
crown of horns the man wears, for we now know that the
horn was the universal symbol of the moon in the primitive world, probably because the shape of the horn is
reminiscent of the crescent shape of the new moon. Similar

horned figures can be found in paintings from all the ancient civilizations of Asia Minor, from Babylonia, Egypt, Greece, Rome, England, Africa, and even the Americas.

The ruins of a large temple at Ur in the ancient Middle East are especially interesting in this regard, since that city is now known to have been the seat of worship for the moon god in Biblical Mesopotamia. Those familiar with the Old Testament may recall that the patriarch Abraham was said to have lived in Ur of the Chaldees, and it is believed by many scholars that ancient Ur and Abraham's Ur of the Chaldees were one and the same. It thus seems likely that at one time in his early years, Abraham and his family may have been worshipers of the moon god before they adopted the god of the Old Testament. Reminders of this old devotion to the moon on the part of the early Hebrews are still preserved in Judaism. In fact, many of the festivals of this religion are intimately associated with certain phases of the moon. The Jewish Passover, for example, is celebrated at the full moon. The Jewish year is likewise founded on the lunar month, but leap years have been interposed, so that with the introduction of an extra month, the calendar is made to conform with the solar year once every nineteen years.

Although the moon is still an object of fascination for modern man, many of us in the twentieth century know very little about its movements or why it changes in shape and color as it does. These movements and changes, however, play an important part in the influences, tangible or otherwise, which the moon exerts upon the earth and many of its inhabitants. Therefore, a brief review of some of the facts and fantasies concerning our nearest celestial neighbor would seem in order.

The moon is actually an 81,000,000,000,000,000,000-ton satellite revolving around the earth. It has a diameter of approximately 2,160 miles (compared to 7,920 miles for the earth), and it is positioned about 239,000 miles away from the earth. At one time, astronomers believed that the moon, the sun, and the earth and the other planets were originally all one large gas cloud. According to the theory, the gas cloud contracted, and gave off materials which later condensed to form the planets and their moons. A second theory proposed by George Darwin, son of the famous biologist Charles Darwin, held that the earth was once a rapidly rotating mass of molten matter and that the moon separated from this mass as a result of centrifugal force. However, on July 20, 1969, U.S. astronauts Neil A. Armstrong and Edwin E. Aldren, Jr., of the space craft Apollo 11, landed on the moon and brought back evidence which showed both theories to be incorrect. A few days after these first humans walked upon the surface of the moon their space craft began its return journey to the earth, carrying with it something which it had not carried on its initial journey— forty-eight pounds of moon rocks, many of which were about 3.5 billion years old. Since this historic flight, there have been more visits to the moon and many more rocks have been returned to our planet. Examination of these rocks has indicated that they bear no resemblance to any rock material found on earth. Consequently, the idea that the earth and the moon evolved from a common source is not supported by geological evidence. While scientists are still at a loss to explain the origins of the moon, thanks to the recent American space program, they now know where not to look in the search for the moon's mysterious past.

The moon is maintained in its orbit around the earth by the same physical principles which allow man-made satellites to remain in orbit. However, because it is much larger than these man-made satellites, the moon produces, and is subject to, effects that are much more dramatic as far as our own planet is concerned.

For one thing, the moon produces no light of its

own. Instead, it merely reflects the sun's rays back to the earth, even though the sun has disappeared beyond the earth's horizon. From the earth, the moon appears totally illuminated only when it is opposite the sun, with the earth in an intermediate position. But even then, it reflects only about 7 percent of the sunlight that falls upon it. On the other hand, when the moon is between the sun and the earth, only the side of the moon that is invisible to the earth is illuminated. The side facing the earth appears completely dark. In between these two extremes, various proportions of the moon appear illuminated. These proportions are called phases and typically are divided into the new and full moon and first and last quarters.

When the moon is "full," we observe the pale and silvery fullness of its glory, rising in the east, reaching its highest point over the earth around midnight, and then slowly setting in the west. Even though the intensity of the light directed at the earth by the full moon is still only 1/500,000 that of the sun, in many parts of the world it was once believed that sleeping in the light of the full moon would weaken the sight. Sailors who slept on deck at night, for example, used to cover their faces during the full moon because they were convinced that they would suffer partial day blindness if moonlight fell upon them.

Continuing in its elliptical orbit around the earth from its position directly opposite the sun, the moon begins to move toward the sun, and as it does so, it begins to "wane," growing apparently smaller and smaller as it reflects less and less of the sun's rays. Finally, it passes between the earth and the sun. In this position, the face of the moon receiving the sun's rays is almost completely invisible to us. At this time, when the moon appears slightly above or below the sun, it is said to be in conjunction. This is the time of the new moon. If, however, instead of moving slightly above or below the sun, the moon should happen to pass right between the sun and

the earth, a solar eclipse takes place. We will return to
this phenomenon in a moment.

When the moon is on its way to becoming a full moon
once again, some speak of it figuratively as "waxing" or
"growing." When it is half grown—that is, when it is a
"half moon," at right angles to the sun and earth and on
its way to becoming a full moon—it is said to be in its
first quarter. After it has become a full moon and is beginning to grow smaller in appearance, the moon is often
spoken of as "dying" or "waning." During this decrease,
when the moon is again at right angles to the sun and
it is a half moon once more, it is said to be in its third
or last quarter.

The rhythmic changing of the moon has not only been
the source of inspiration to poets and writers throughout
the ages, it has also been the source of many of the nursery
rhymes which we teach our children. For instance, in
the rhyme:

> Jack and Jill went up the hill
> To fetch a pail of water;
> Jack fell down and broke his crown,
> And Jill came tumbling after.

can be found the roots of an ancient allusion to the
moon. The fall of Jack and the subsequent "tumbling
after" of Jill both represent the waning disappearance of
the moon. The names of Jack and Jill are also of interest,
for the name "Jack" is derived from a verb meaning "to
get bigger, to expand, or increase," while the name "Jill"
comes from a verb meaning "to break into pieces, to
dissolve, to get smaller." Hence, the two characters in
the rhyme are essentially personifications of the waxing
and waning of the moon. The pail of water also has a
deeper significance, since the moon was once universally
connected with rainfall and dew, as will be discussed
in a later chapter. The comings and goings of the moon
thus extend into areas of human imagination that often

go beyond our recognition and expectation.

The color of the moon, as well as its shape, undergo periodic transformations. For instance, when the moon is high in the sky it has a familiar silvery appearance, but when it is near the horizon, it sometimes looks "blood red." These color changes are due to the interaction of the moon's light with the earth's atmosphere.

To understand this phenomenon, one must first know that while light appears white, it is actually a mixture of all the colors of the rainbow. Light itself is made up of electromagnetic waves that travel through space like ripples on a pond. When the light waves are very short, the light appears bluish. When they are long, the light appears reddish. The colors green and yellow have wavelengths intermediate between those associated with blue and red. White light is simply a combination of all these wavelengths.

The appearance of a red moon is due to the fact that the short and medium wavelengths of blue, green, and yellow do not reach us from the moon on some days. This can happen when there are air particles in the atmosphere which scatter these short and medium wavelengths in all directions. If enough of these wavelengths get scattered, the light that penetrates the earth's atmosphere and reaches our eyes is composed of the long waves characteristic of red. At the horizon, the light reflected from the moon has to pass through much more atmosphere to get to our eyes than when the moon is directly overhead. At such times, more of the short wavelengths of light get scattered than when the moon is directly overhead, and therefore when the moon begins to emerge over the horizon, it often has a "blood red" appearance.

Before leaving the subject of moonlight, we must not fail to mention that most romantic moon of all, the harvest moon. As a result of its elliptical orbit around the earth, the moon rises and sets about forty minutes later on each successive day of the year, although the duration of this

period varies considerably according to the position of
the moon relative to the equator. Around the time of
the autumn equinox in September, the extra light from the
full moon supposedly provides additional hours for the
farmer to gather his crops before winter sets in. This
full moon, which is associated with harvest time, has thus
appropriately been dubbed the harvest moon.

The cycle from full moon to full moon takes 29½
days and is referred to as a synodic month. A question
may arise in the minds of some readers at this point,
inasmuch as the moon's cycle is generally thought to be
28 days.

The 28-day period is actually an average of the synodic
month and the sidereal month. The latter refers to the
time it takes the moon to make one complete revolution
around the earth—27 1/3 days. This sidereal month is
shorter than the synodic month because it takes a shorter
time for the moon to pass completely around the earth
than it does for it to go from one full moon to another.
The reason is that the earth itself is moving around the
sun. Since full moons occur only when the moon is
directly opposite the sun with the earth in between, the
moon must travel farther from one full moon to the next
in order to compensate for the added distance that the
earth has moved during this time.

In each year, there are about 12 7/9 synodic months.
Since the number of synodic months per year is not exact,
the time for each lunar phase advances by about eleven
days each year. After a period of nineteen years, this
difference is tantamount to seven complete synodic
months, and the lunar phases reoccur on the same days
as they did nineteen years before. This nineteen-year
cycle is especially important to the Christian calendar,
as it constitutes the basis for the date for Easter Sunday,
this being the first Sunday after the Spring equinox
(March 21) after the full moon.

The fact that the moon's orbit around the earth is

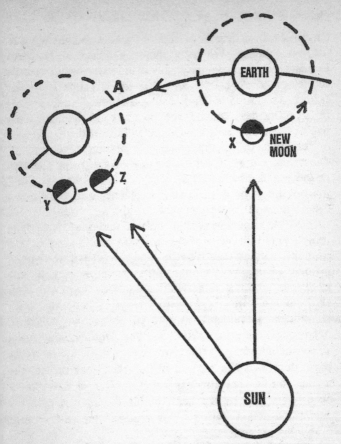

Explanation of Sidereal and Synodic Months: At X, the Moon is aligned with both the Sun and the Earth and we see a New Moon. The Moon, however, is constantly revolving about the Earth every 27⅓ days. When the Moon is back in position Y, it has completed one revolution around the Earth. This is known as a Sidereal Month. However, while the Moon has been revolving around the Earth, the Earth has been revolving around the Sun. In the diagram, the letter A represents the distance covered by the Earth in 27⅓ days. Because the Earth has moved, the Sun, Earth, and Moon are no longer aligned at position Y. For alignment to occur, the Moon must continue to orbit the Earth until it is at position Z. To go from X to Z takes 29½ days, a period known as the Synodic Month.

elliptical rather than circular also explains why it appears to change in size. When the moon is closest to the earth (at its *perigee*), it is about 221,000 miles away; when it is farthest away (at its *apogee*), the distance from the earth to the moon is about 253,000 miles. This difference of 32,000 miles accounts for the apparent change in the size of the moon as it travels around the earth.

For much of our understanding of the movements of the moon, we are indebted to one of the great geniuses of the world, Sir Isaac Newton. In 1665, when England was in the grip of the bubonic plague, and the "black death" forced the closing of the country's various universities, Newton, who was then only a young student, suddenly found himself on vacation. It was during this respite from his studies that Newton observed the now famous incident of the apple falling to the ground and, as he put it, "began to think of gravitation as extending to the orb of the moon." In 1687, twenty-two years later, this train of thought culminated in one of the most important scientific works ever written. Entitled *Mathematical Principles of Natural Philosophy*, Newton's epoch-making book described the movements of the moon in mathematical terms, and also explained why these movements occurred at all. At the heart of his theory was the universal law of gravitation which remains one of the basic principles of modern-day physics.

According to Newton's law, every particle in the universe exerts an attraction on every other particle. In theory, therefore, each speck of dust exerts a pull on every object in the world, just as every object exerts a pull on that speck of dust. However, the force of that pull depends on two factors—the distance between each object and the mass of each object. The attraction between a car and a speck of dust is thus not very great because even though they are very near one another, the mass of the car and especially the mass of the speck of dust are insignificant compared to the pull that the earth exerts on an object.

The attraction between the earth and the moon, however, is very substantial, owing to the large mass of each sphere and the relatively small distance that separates them. Although the sun has a mass that is many million times greater than that of the moon, it is also many millions of miles farther away. Therefore the factor of mass is countered by the factor of distance. Nevertheless, the sun still exerts a considerable attraction on the earth.

The law of gravitation provides an explanation for the influence of the moon on the rise and fall of the oceanic tides. For example, while the earth's continents are solid and therefore cannot be pulled very much (measurements using very complicated equipment have determined that the actual extent of the stretch is about nine inches), the oceans have much more flexibility. As a result, the oceans are attracted to a much greater extent by the gravitational pull of celestial bodies such as the moon. Because of the law of gravitation, the moon tends to pull the waters of the ocean toward it, and the part of the ocean directly opposite the moon is pulled the strongest, making it form a kind of bulge. As the earth rotates, this bulge moves with it. If the earth were entirely covered with water, this bulge would never be noticed. Because of the land, however, the bulging of the water eventually gets nearer to the beach and the water begins to creep ashore (high tide). If the shore has a very gradual slope, the ocean may even advance rather far inland.

Once the earth has rotated to the point that the moon is no longer above the sea the gravitational pull on the ocean is lessened, the bulge no longer occurs, and the water begins to recede (low tide).

If the moon were stationary and only the earth moved, the tides in any one place would always occur at the

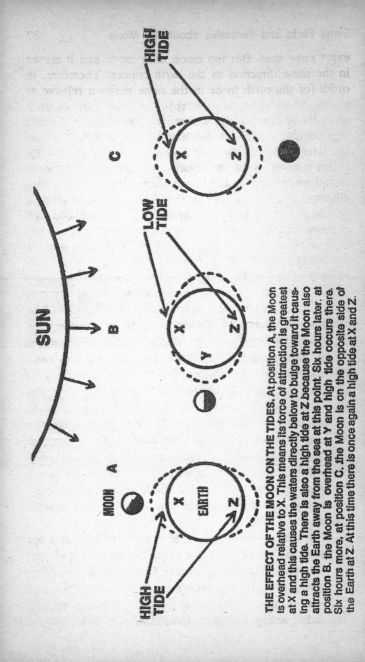

THE EFFECT OF THE MOON ON THE TIDES. At position A, the Moon is overhead relative to X. This means its force of attraction is greatest at X and this causes the waters directly below to bulge toward it causing a high tide. There is also a high tide at Z because the Moon also attracts the Earth away from the sea at this point. Six hours later, at position B, the Moon is overhead at Y and high tide occurs there. Six hours more, at position C, the Moon is on the opposite side of the Earth at Z. At this time there is once again a high tide at X and Z.

exact same time. But the moon does move and it moves in the same direction as the earth rotates. Therefore, in order for the earth to be in the same position relative to the moon each day, it must rotate a little extra. Since it takes the earth about 24 hours and fifty minutes to make one complete rotation and then catch up to the moon, the tides occur a little later every day in any given area.

But the story is still not quite complete. Since the moon is not stationary, but revolves around the earth in an elliptical orbit, it is closer to the earth at some times than at others. Consequently, the gravitational attraction which it exerts on the earth when it is closest to our planet (i.e., at its perigee) is greater than when it is farther away in its elliptical orbit (*i.e.*, at its apogee).

In addition, there is still another influence to consider—the sun. The effect of the sun on the tides varies only slightly as the earth rotates on its axis from night to day. Because of its enormous mass, the sun exerts a tremendous pull on the earth even at a distance of 93,000,000 miles, but this pull is relatively constant. As the earth rotates, the hourly variation in the sun's attraction for any particular geographic region is negligible. Nevertheless, the sun does have some influence on the tides, an influence which becomes especially noticeable when the sun's gravitational force pulls in the same or in opposite direction to the moon, a condition referred to as a *syzygy*. During the time of the new and the full moon when such syzygies occur, the combined gravitational forces summate and the oceans pound high against the sea cliffs and move farther up the beaches. These two periods of maximal tidal movement are called the spring tides, although they have nothing at all to do with the time of season that they occur. When the moon is at its first or third (last) quarter, however, the gravitational pull of the sun and the moon are at right angles to one another. Instead of acting in concert, their effects are now opposed.

Consequently, the tides are much lower. This latter tidal period is referred to as the neap tides.

The highest tides occur when the moon is both at syzygy with the sun and at its perigee with respect to the earth. Conversely, the lowest tides occur when the moon is both in its first or third quarters and at its apogee.

Not all the waters of the earth exhibit the tidal phenomenon, however. Nor are the tidal movements uniform where they do occur. In order for the waters on the earth to rise and fall, they must have freedom of movement. But this is hardly possible in the case of the lakes, since their surrounding land masses severely restrict any such movement. This restriction also accounts for a tidal movement that is barely perceptible in the Mediterranean sea, in spite of the fact that it is a rather large body of water.

If you glance at a map, you will see that the Mediterranean Sea is bounded by land on all of its sides except for the narrow straits of Gibraltar where it meets the Atlantic Ocean. Because of the narrowness of this opening, the bulge of water which begins in the Atlantic cannot move very quickly into the Mediterranean. Before any relatively large quantity can enter, the earth rotates past the point where the bulge is trying to get through the strait and thus leaves it behind. As a result, high tides do not occur in the Mediterranean Sea.

Although tides still do occur in landlocked water bodies, they are of such negligible proportions that special equipment is required to demonstrate their existence. In contrast, the waters of the large oceans such as the Atlantic and the Pacific are quite free to move and their tides are consequently quite appreciable. For example, in the Bay of Fundy which lies between Nova Scotia and New Brunswick in Canada, the tides can rise as much as fifty to sixty feet; this represents approximately 100 billion tons of water rising and falling in the bay.

Thus, while the pull of the moon on the earth is rela-

Consequently the tides are much lower. This latter tidal period is referred to as the neap tides.

The highest tides occur when the moon is both at syzygy and at perigee.

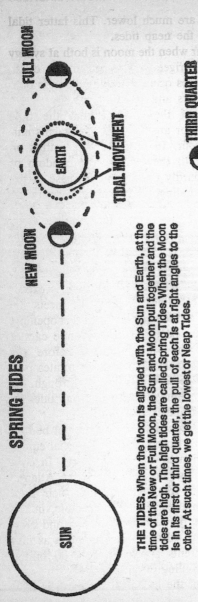

SPRING TIDES

NEAP TIDES

FULL MOON

NEW MOON

TIDAL MOVEMENT

EARTH

THIRD QUARTER

FIRST QUARTER

TIDAL MOVEMENT

EARTH

SUN

SUN

THE TIDES. When the Moon is aligned with the Sun and Earth, at the time of the New or Full Moon, the Sun and Moon pull together and the tides are high. The high tides are called Spring Tides. When the Moon is in its first or third quarter, the pull of each is at right angles to the other. At such times, we get the lowest or Neap Tides.

tively the same at all points of the globe, the effect of
the attraction is highly dependent upon local geographical
conditions. The contrast between the tides in the Mediterranean Sea and the Bay of Fundy are proof enough
of that. To give another such illustration, just consider
the tides on either side of the Panama Canal. On the
Atlantic side, the tides rise no more than one to two
feet. On the Pacific side, only forty miles away, the tides
rise twelve to sixteen feet! The gravitational force of
the moon may thus start our oceans moving, but the
actual degree to which they rise and fall will depend
upon where in the world these movements are occurring.

The incoming tide in an area is known as the flood
tide; the outgoing tide is referred to as the ebb tide. These
tidal movements are of particular importance for the
countless numbers of people who derive their living from
the sea or who simply enjoy living or visiting nearby.
At flood tide, when the waves wash far up the shore,
objects that were clearly visible only a few hours before
may be completely submerged; small boats that were
grounded may be freed and carried out to sea if they
were not securely anchored. At these times too, large
ships are able to enter or leave otherwise inaccessible
harbors. When the tide begins to ebb, objects on the
beach once again may become grounded and larger
vessels must remain far out from shore. Along the
beaches, the ebb tide may have left behind little tide
pools in among the rocks, and stranded in these tiny
pools are often small fish and crabs that cannot leave
until the next flood tide releases them from these prisons.

The behavior of a number of animals that inhabit the
shore is markedly affected by the rhythm of the tides.
The cycle of the flatworm, *Convoluta*, for instance, is
finely attuned to the rise and fall of the tides. At ebb
tide, these primitive organisms rise out of the sand and
emerge onto the beaches to bask in the warmth of the
sun. As the tide begins to rise again, however, the worm

returns to its burrow to escape being washed out to sea by the incoming waves.

In 1953, Dr. Frank Brown and his colleagues reported the sensitivity of another marine animal, the crab, to the tidal cycle. These curious creatures were actually seen to turn different colors depending on whether it was high or low tide!

Clams, crabs, oysters, snails, and a whole host of other marine animals are now being intensively studied by naturalists and biologists to determine how and why these primitive creatures show such a sensitivity to the rise and fall of the sea. One interesting discovery to come out of this work is that many of these animals show the same tidal rhythm even when they are removed from the ocean beaches to the sand of laboratory aquariums where there are no tides. Apparently, in the course of evolution, these animals have developed a kind of sixth sense that tells them when the tides should rise and fall. Even when they are taken from their natural habitats, this sixth sense tells them that it is time to come out of the sand to lie in the sun, or to change color, or to begin to feed, or to remain burrowed in the sand until such time as would be appropriate for their emergence.

The rhythm of life associated with the tides has no doubt led superstitious minds to connect the rise and fall of the seas with human fortunes as well, as illustrated by these medieval verses:

> Tyde flowing is feared, for many a thing,
> Great danger to such as be sick it doth bring.
> Sea ebb, by long ebbing, some respite it doth give,
> And sendeth good comfort, to such as shall live.

Readers familiar with Dickens' *David Copperfield* will likewise be reminded of this superstition in the exchange between David and Mr. Peggotty concerning the death of old Barkis:

"He's a-going out with the tide," said Mr. Peggotty to me, behind his hand.

My eyes were dim, and so were Mr. Peggotty's, but I repeated in a whisper, "With the tide?"

"People can't die along the coast," said Mr. Peggotty, "except when the tides pretty nigh out. They can't be born unless its pretty nigh in—not properly born, till flood. He's a-going out with the tide. It's ebb at half-arter three, slack water half an hour. If he lives till it turns, he'll hold his own till past the flood, and go out with the next tide."

The origins of this strange idea that the tides and human life were inextricably linked is not difficult to imagine, given the importance of the flood and ebb of the tides to seafaring peoples around the world. The flood tide marked the fullness of the sea, the time when boats would float high in the water. It was the coming in of the sea and could be likened to a beginning, hence its association with birth and the continuance of life. The ebb tide, on the other hand, signaled the emptying of the shore and the fall of the sea, and could be likened to an ending, hence its association with death. To people dependent on the sea for their livelihood, the rise and fall of the tides understandably became a metaphor for the beginning and end of human life and with time and frequent usage, the metaphor eventually evolved into a superstitious conviction.

Let us return now to the subject of eclipses, events in which the sun is obscured by the moon (solar eclipse) or the moon is shaded by the earth (lunar eclipse). The former has the effect of blocking off the sun's light and is caused whenever the moon comes between the earth and the sun. A lunar eclipse, on the other hand, occurs when the earth comes between the sun and the moon, thereby preventing the moon from reflecting the sun's rays. At such times both the moon and the earth are in complete darkness.

Oddly enough, lunar eclipses at one time produced

much more excitement and fear than did solar eclipses. According to the Greek historian Plutarch, most of the people of ancient Greece were relatively unperturbed at solar eclipses. But a great alarm was often heard whenever the moon unexpectedly disappeared, as such an occurrence was considered to be a heavenly harbinger of some great misfortune on earth. The Roman naturalist Pliny comments that in his day (first century A.D.) most men believed that these lunar eclipses were brought on by witchcraft. To break the evil spell, it was not an uncommon practice for people to shout and make loud noises so as to frighten the evil spirits away. According to anthropologists, these same beliefs and practices are still current in many primitive tribes around the world for much the same reason.

Eclipses of the moon have also played an important part in history. In 168 B.C., for example, on the day before the Roman armies crushed the last of the Greek forces of Macedonia, the Roman commander informed his men of an imminent lunar eclipse and of its natural causes. When the eclipse happened just as he predicted, the Roman soldiers marveled at the wisdom of their leader and their spirits were considerably lifted. The Greek soldiers, however, were unprepared for the eclipse. As they watched the moon disappear, they interpreted the event as a sign of their defeat and an omen that their kingdom was about to fall. As a result, their confidence sagged, and morale was low when they went into battle the next day. Without the will to win, they were soundly defeated.

It is also well known that Christopher Columbus was saved from death by his prediction of a lunar eclipse. This event occurred on March 1, 1509. During his last expedition to the New World, Columbus and his men were captured by a group of natives and were imprisoned and reduced to starvation by their captors. Aware that an eclipse of the moon was about to take place, Columbus threatened to deprive these natives of the light of the moon unless they brought him food and released him and his men. At first the natives ignored his threat. But when the moon was eclipsed on that very night, they became exceedingly frightened. In their fear they released Columbus and brought him a supply of food, begging only that the explorer bring back the moon, which, of course, he promised to do.

In these and related legends and curios of the past, we see how the ancestors of modern man throughout the world have looked upon the moon and wondered at its regularly recurring pattern of growth and decay and have sought to understand the relationship between these changes and their own mysterious and recurring cycle of birth and death.

Thus far we have examined many facts and fantasies about the moon. These fantasies are looked upon as more than just amusing products of the human mind, however, by anthropologists and other social scientists, who see in these myths and stories, the raw material out of which modern science and religion eventually emerged.

The old physicians of the past also made use of their knowledge of the moon to treat their patients, and some of their observations have been corroborated recently by modern-day medicine. For instance, we now know, thanks to the efforts of Dr. Edson J. Andrews, whose research was mention in the previous chapter, that as once believed, the amount of bleeding in postoperative surgery is significantly affected by the phase of the moon.

The rediscovery of such relationships by modern scientific analysis has opened up an entirely new area for medical thought. With this sobering revelation in mind, let us examine some other erstwhile "superstitions," now shown to be scientific truths, about the moon's influence on birth, growth, decay, and death, in plants, in animals, and in man's life itself.

DURING the winter, Pacific Grove, California (otherwise known as Butterfly Town, U.S.A.), is the scene of one of the most magnificent sights in all of nature—the annual migration of the graceful monarch butterfly. From their summer habitats all over the United States and Canada, millions and millions of these beautiful orange-and-black creatures make the long journey to take up residence in the city's wind-sheltered groves of pine and eucalyptus trees. There they rest contentedly during the cool hours of the morning. As the day gets warmer, however, the monarchs rouse themselves from their sleep and soon begin fluttering and flitting from flower to flower in search of food and nourishment in their private winter vacationland. Then, as the winter turns to spring and the daylight hours grow longer and longer, the acres and acres of butterflies bid adieu to the hospitality of Pacific Grove's residents and set out on the exhausting flight back to the different places from which they originally came. It is a cycle that has gone on for as long as anyone can remember and will probably keep on happening as long as there are monarch butterflies in North America.

45

On the other side of the world, another event has been
repeating itself for countless years—the breeding cycle
of the emperor penguin. During the Fall, thousands and
thousands of these comical-looking birds begin waddling
and swimming across the barren icy regions of the Ant-
arctic as they make their way to their far-off breeding
grounds. There the male and female penguins mate and
build their nests. Next the female lays her egg, and then
she leaves the male to keep it warm while she returns
once more to the distant shore for food. Now she begins
to gorge herself with shrimp while her husband patiently
and trustingly maintains his vigil on the nest, growing
hungrier and hungrier by the day. When finally he and
the chick, which he alone has hatched, are just about to
die of starvation, the female returns and regurgitates the
food she has stored within her to her faithful consort and
her new infant offspring.

Scenarios such as the annual migration of the butterfly,
the emperor penguin, and countless other inhabitants
of our earth have been going on for time immemorial.
Such cyclic activity is, in fact, one of the fundamental
characteristics of a great many animals. But why should
birds and insects migrate south in winter and north in
summer? What signals set these cycles into motion?
Obviously many of them are brought about by changes
in temperature and hours of daylight. The marvelous
and intriguing synchronization of animal behavior and
the weather is something we have always been aware of,
but it is only recently that the phenomenon itself has
begun to be appreciated by our scientists.

Our planet earth exhibits its own 365-day cycle in
its orbit around the sun, during which it passes through
a recurring seasonal pattern of spring, summer, fall and
winter. During this procession through the seasons, seeds
germinate, plants grow, flowers bloom, and then these
plants die or become dormant. In the spring, animals
such as the bear come out of their caves and roam the

parks and forests in search of food. They mate and have cubs. Then as fall begins, they start storing up enormous quantities of food in their bodies and search out dens, which they furnish with evergreen boughs. With the coming of winter they hibernate and go into a long undisturbed sleep. In the spring, the whole cycle starts anew.

We humans also have our annual cycles. In 1972, Dr. Franz Halberg and his associates at the University of Minnesota's Chronobiology Laboratories used a computer to analyze data which they gathered from various U.S. vital statistics publications and from the World Health Organization. The analysis indicated, among other things, that most deaths due to heart disease occur in the month of January. Winter is also the season in which most people catch colds, even those living in the balmy climate of Florida. Another curious finding was that the greatest number of suicides occur in the months of April, May, and June. In some mysterious way, it was clearly evident that human behavior and human physiology are clearly in tune with the seasons.

Besides journeying around the sun, the earth also rotates on its axis once every twenty-four hours, giving rise to a light/dark cycle, which is sometimes referred to as a circadian rhythm. This term is derived from two Latin words, *circa*, meaning around, and *dies*, meaning day. When scientists speak of circadian rhythms, they mean cycles which tend to repeat themselves approximately once every twenty-four hours.

Anyone who has ever had a garden or raised plants indoors knows that flowers tend to open their petals during the day and close them at night and that the leaves of a plant stand upright and extended when they are bathed in light but droop when darkness enshrouds them. These changes are simply indications of the plant's circadian rhythms. Rodents such as the mouse and the rat also have circadian rhythms, but unlike plants, they tend to be more active during the night than during the daylight hours. Although it is now known that these rhythms persist even when plants and animals are raised under constant environmental conditions, the timing of these cycles more often than not tends to conform rather than remain independent of the rhythms of the universe.

We humans, of course, live by the twenty-four-hour cycle of the sun. When the sun comes over the horizon and chases away the night, it is morning, time to get up and have breakfast and go to work. When the sun is directly overhead, it is noon, time for lunch. As the sun begins to drop behind the western horizon, we leave our jobs and head for home and supper. A few hours of darkness, and it's time for bed.

Not only is human behavior synchronized to the sun, the biological rhythms of the human body also take their cues from light and temperature changes that emanate from that celestial furnace.

How often must we tend to toiletry needs at night compared with during the day? Experiments have shown that even when people live underground, their urinary cycles can be shortened or lengthened depending on whether the illumination is made brighter or dimmer. The female menstrual cycle, as we shall see in a later chapter, can be markedly shortened by sleeping with a night light on. Another interesting phenomenon that may or may not be related to the effects of light on the female menstrual rhythm is the twenty-four-hour cycle in the rate of human births.

Briefly stated, the highest frequency of human births, not only in North America but in Western Europe as well, occurs at night between the hours of 9:00 P.M. and 9:00 A.M., with the peak birth rate occurring around 3:00 A.M.

The earliest study of this phenomenon to appear in a scientific journal was reported as far back as 1848, and since then this observation has been corroborated many times.

For example, an analysis of over 16,000 birth records for the city of Birmingham, England, for the years 1951 and 1952, found that 55.6 percent of all reported births in that city occurred between 9:00 P.M. and 9:00 A.M., compared with 44.4 percent for the period between 9:00 A.M. to 9:00 P.M. The fewest number of births during any day occurred between 1:00 and 2:00 P.M. Similar results have also been reported for Lancashire, England.

In Oklahoma City, Oklahoma, an examination of 38,668 hospital births over a five-year period revealed a 9.6 percent increase in the number of babies born during the night. An analysis of over 4,000 births in a New York hospital corroborated previous reports of a peak birth frequency between 2:00 and 4:00 A.M. Likewise, an analysis of over a half-million births revealed a distinct peak birth rate around 3:00 A.M., with the lowest number of births occurring between 1:00 and 8:00 P.M.

It is thus abundantly clear from these and many additional studies that the frequency of human births during the day is not random but is governed by some systematic influence. Whether this diurnal periodicity is due to some particular effect of the sun is still quite problematical. The possibility, however, should not be discounted.

Although we like to think of ourselves as masters of our universe, we are in reality prisoners of an endless multitude of extraterrestrial forces like the light and heat of the sun. It's true we can now travel to the moon and send rockets to Mercury or Venus or other far-off planets, but can we change the weather? We can irrigate deserts, grow crops where only dry hot sand once covered the land, but can we exist without rain?

All living things, from the lowest form of plant life to man, depend for existence on the extraterrestrial influence of the sun. From a distance of 93,000,000 miles, the sun gives us energy in the form of light and heat. This energy is used by plants to grow and to make the oxygen that we breathe. Without the sun, plants would die, and even if we could manufacture oxygen by some other means, all the animals that depended on plants for food would cease to exist. And without plants or animals, human life could not continue. Our fate and the fate of our planet thus depend on the energy we receive from a distant extraterrestrial globe. This globe is not even a solid mass. Instead it is made up of extremely hot gases that are kept under such pressure that they have greater density than any known substance on earth.

While heat and light are obvious extraterrestrial influences we receive from the sun, they are by no means the only such influences to reach our planet. In addition to the light we can see and the heat we can feel, the sun also bombards us with invisible kinds of energy such as ultraviolet and infrared light, and X-rays and gamma rays. Sometimes, however, nuclear reactions going on within our sun become so violent that its surface seems to erupt like a volcano and immense electromagnetic energy is shot out into space. At such times, radio communication on earth becomes disrupted because of changes which this energy causes in the earth's magnetic field when it ultimately reaches our planet.

These solar eruptions, which are actually giant magnetic cyclones, are called sunspots, and they appear as dark patches on the surface of the sun. Some of these sunspots measure about 60 billion square miles, an area equivalent to about 300 times the surface of the earth.

Although sunspot activity goes on all the time, every eleven years there is a dramatic increase in the frequency of these eruptions. At such times not only are our radio signals disrupted, but plant growth also appears to be affected. According to the *Bulletin Astronomique de France*, the quality of French burgundy wine is at its best every eleven years coincident with the height of the solar sunspot activity, whereas during the years of low solar sunspot activity, the vintage is relatively poor. Not only are vineyards sensitive to these extraterrestrial effects, tree growth is also dramatically affected as evident from examination of their concentric rings pattern in which the eleven-year cycle is clearly visible. In Russia, the coming and going of locust plagues has been shown to follow the eleven-year sunspot cycle. In the Caspian Sea, the breeding activity of the sturgeon is at its height once every eleven years and coincides exactly with the sunspot cycle. At such times masses and masses of sturgeons are in a frenzy to reproduce, and then having exhausted themselves in their sexual bouts, they die blissfully of their wanton passion.

At the University of Moscow, Professor A. L. Tchijevsky has conducted exhaustive studies of the relationship between sunspot activity and the occurrence of wars, revolution, migrations, epidemics, etc. from 500 B.C. to 1900 A.D. and has found that 72 percent of these social upheavals have coincided with the peaks of solar flareups. Apparently we humans tend to become excitable during the years of intensive sunspot activity, and this excitability takes the form of social unrest.

Diseases also seem to flourish during increased solar activity. The great diptheria and cholera plagues that ravaged Europe, the typhus epidemic in Russia, and even the outbreak of smallpox that devastated Chicago all were found to coincide with the eleven-year sunspot cycle. This increased susceptibility may be due to changes in the body's immunity system, since the number of lymphocytes, or white blood cells, is greatly reduced during periods of increased solar eruptions. The regular pattern of epidemics is no longer with us, however, thanks to the successful medical advances that have recently been made in the treatment of infectious diseases. Nevertheless, it is still the case that there are more instances of heart attacks during periods of increased solar activity than during those times that our sun is relatively "quiet."

Next to the sun, the extraterrestrial influence that most

affects the earth is our nearest celestial neighbor, the moon. We have already seen how the moon affects the rise and fall of the seas, and in the pages that follow, we will see that the moon controls not only the seas and its inhabitants, but also more complex creatures, including man himself. But before we examine these hitherto neglected areas of scientific study, let us consider briefly the moon's influence on some of the more primitive creatures that inhabit our earth.

The sun is not the only cosmic body that can synchronize behavioral and physiological cycles in living organisms. Because of its influence on the tides, the moon sets into motion the biological rhythms of many of the creatures that live by the seashore. However, there are also many marine animals whose cycles are not triggered by the tides but instead are set in motion directly by the moon. One of the first animals for which this was shown to be the case was the lowly oyster.

The oyster (*Ostrea virginica*) is a member of the mollusc family, which also includes snails, clams, mussels, scallops, squids, and octopuses. Its breeding or spawning season occurs during the summer months, at which time a single oyster may produce as many as half a billion eggs! When it is in this condition, the oyster takes on a rather stringy and watery appearance and many connoisseurs of shellfish claim that much of the oyster's flavor is lost at this time. It is probably because of this change in appearance and flavor that the totally erroneous idea arose that oysters are poisonous if eaten during the R-less, or summer, months, from May to August.

Although the oyster produces an enormous quantity of eggs, most of these are eaten by other marine animals before they hatch. Even should they be fortunate enough not to be swallowed by other inhabitants of the shore, the oyster larvae, called spat, are still at the mercy of the ocean, and most of them are carried aimlessly up and down the beach with the waves. Some of these spat, however, do manage to remain in the muddy estuaries where rivers deposit their silt as they enter the seas. Here they drop to the bottom at the ebb tide and patiently await the return of the flood tide so that they can be carried farther upstream. After each brief journey they settle to the bottom once again to wait for another wave. Slowly but surely, with the aid of the rise and fall of the ocean, they are carried along the estuary, until finally they reach a suitable resting ground where they can attach themselves to a rock or some other oyster. Once they do so, however, they are doomed to spend the rest of their lives riveted to that same spot, since the mortarlike substance which they secrete at such times creates what for them is an unbreakable cement bond.

The term "mollusc" itself means "soft" and refers to the fragile body of marine animals like the oyster. Members of the mollusc family, however, develop a hard outer shell which they use to protect themselves against their enemies and the various materials that the ocean carries about in its innards. These shells of armor are called valves, and there may be only one of them, such as that which covers the snail, or two, such as those which enclose the oyster, in which case they are called bivalves.

The bivalve shell is joined together at one edge by a huge ligament controlled by a powerful muscle called the adductor. Collectors of seashells can still see the scar on the inside of the shell where this muscle was once attached if they should happen to come across an oyster that has recently died.

The adductor muscle is responsible for opening and closing the oyster's bivalves. Marine biologists have long been aware that oysters open their shells at high tide in order to filter nourishment from the sea and close them when the tide goes out to keep from drying out. It has been estimated that a single oyster filters as much as eighteen gallons of water and eats as many as 72,000,000 organisms per day during the time between flood and ebb tides.

At first it was believed that the rhythmic pattern of opening and closing of the oyster's bivalves was triggered by the movements of the tide and therefore was only secondarily influenced by the moon. According to the accepted theory, the oyster sensed that the flood tide was upon it because of the water pressure or some other such stimulus and opened its jaws accordingly; when the ocean was at ebb tide, the stimulus disappeared and this became a signal for the oyster to close up shop. But Dr. Frank A. Brown, a biologist at Northwestern University in Evanston, Illinois, had an inkling that more was involved than merely the oyster's reflex responding to the rise and fall of the tides.

What would happen to this rhythm, he asked himself, if the oyster were removed from its natural habitat and were placed in an environment 1,000 miles away from the ocean? Without the stimulus of the tides, would the oyster keep its shells closed permanently?

To find out, Dr. Brown had a batch of fifteen oysters shipped to him in Evanston from New Haven, Connecticut. Once they arrived at his laboratory, he put them in glass vessels and kept them under dim illumination. Next, he tied one end of a thread to each oyster's upper shell and tied the other end to a lever-operated recording pen which allowed him to monitor the opening and closing movements of each oyster automatically and continuously.

At first the oysters still continued to open and close as if they were back home in Connecticut. Thus, even without the tides, the oysters still exhibited a cyclic opening and closing of their shells identical to that which was still occurring in the oysters back on the Atlantic seacoast. Possibly the oysters had retained some kind of memory of when the tides were supposed to come in and go out, since they had gone through the same routine many many times before.

But then, two weeks after being brought to Evanston, something interesting began to happen. Instead of opening and closing in time with the tides that still washed their native estuaries in far-off Connecticut, the oysters began to open and close three hours later in the day and continued to do so after that. Apparently there was some other stimulus besides the tides that was triggering this activity. But what could this signal be? The oysters were housed in dim illumination, so the signal couldn't be light. The laboratory was temperature- and pressure-controlled, so those factors had been eliminated. It was uncanny. The only other possibility was that the same force which affected the tides must also be directly affecting the oysters. Could it be the moon? Dr. Brown reached for his almanac. Sure enough, the oysters were opening and closing in rhythm with the position of the moon relative to Evanston. At such times as there would theoretically have been a high tide in Evanston, if Evanston were on the seacoast, the oysters were opening their shells.

The moon controlled the tides in Connecticut, and if Evanston had been on the ocean, instead of on Lake Michigan, the moon would be controlling its tides as well. But the tides were only a manifestation of the moon's cosmic influence on the earth. They were only the tangible evidence of the moon's directive power over our planet. Without the tides, this visible evidence was not apparent, but this did not mean that it was no longer there. It was only that most scientists had not been aware of its other effects; probably they had not even considered the possibility that there could be an effect of the moon which was not physical in nature. Or if they had considered it, they had not dared to make this consideration known to their colleagues for fear of being ridiculed. And so the anecdotal reports concerning the moon's influence on plants and animals continued to be regarded merely as amusing and superstitious products of gullible minds.

But now there was scientific evidence, irrefutable evidence at that, demonstrating that the moon was directly responsible for the activity cycle of at least one living organism. Dr. Brown now began to ask himself whether there were any other animals that might be directly responsive to the moon. With the enthusiasm and excitement of discovery and anticipation that once spurred the early explorers on to the far reaches of our once mysterious planet, Dr. Brown jetted back to the shores of the Atlantic to study yet another marine animal, the fiddler crab, to see if it too would respond to the movements of the moon.

Fiddler crabs (*Uca pugilata*), so called because of their large claw which looks like a fiddle, spend most of their time burrowed in the sand of our New England beaches. As the tide ebbs, however, these animals emerge from their burrows by the thousands to search for food. The female of the species has two eating claws which it uses to separate silt into edible and nonedible food materials. The edible portion is then brought to its mouth, where it is rinsed free of organic substances, which are then swallowed. The indigestible sediment is then formed into a silt ball and is spit back out onto the beach. Male fiddler crabs go through the same motions, but they have a harder time of it, since they possess only a single eating claw. Their other claw, which is much larger and powerful, is used to fight other males for the privilege of courting the female.

Just before the tide comes in, fiddler crabs abandon their food-getting behavior and quickly scurry back to their holes, plugging the entrance after them with mud. Moments later, the flood tide inundates the beach above them. Since the crabs head for the safety of their burrows before the tide is actually upon them, it was apparent to biologists like Dr. Brown that the sea itself was not the cue which informed the crab that it was time to take shelter. Could it be that this peculiar ability to anticipate the flood tide was prompted by the moon?

Dr. Brown scoured the Atlantic coast to bring back specimens for his laboratory. And once again, 1,000 miles from their native homes, secluded in dark temperature- and pressure-controlled surroundings, the cycle of feeding behavior of the crabs began to coincide with the time of the nonexistent tides in Evanston, Illinois.

Other experiments were also conducted. Would marine animals that had never seen the pale light of the moon or felt the tides also react to the movements of the earth's satellite? To find out, Dr. Brown caught a number of crayfish, species *cavernicola*, in Mammoth Cave, Kentucky, and brought them to his laboratory. These fish had lived all their lives in constant darkness and temperature. They had never been exposed to the light of the sun or the moon, or felt the rise and fall of the tides. Yet they too exhibited a distinct rhythm in their metabolic processes, one that bore an unquestionable relationship to the position of the moon.

Reading of these interesting studies regarding the moon's influence on these various marine animals, other scientists quickly became intrigued and soon began conducting their own experiments along the lines pioneered by Dr. Brown. In one such study, reported by Dr. M. F. Bennett, fiddler crabs were collected from two different beaches where flood tides were four hours apart. Again the animals were kept in a specially designed laboratory that kept environmental conditions constant. On the first day, both groups of crabs exhibited the four-hour difference in their activity cycles that corresponded to the difference in the tidal activity characteristic of their native habitats. But after six to seven days in their new setting, both groups came into synchrony with each other and with the times of the lunar zenith and lunar nadir. The results thus showed that while the tides may play an important role in triggering the behavior of animals such as the crab under natural conditions, in the absence of any tides, their activity cycles become directly synchronized with local lunar events.

According to the detailed studies of various entomologists, scientists whose interests are devoted to the study of insects, there is also a relationship between the activity of many bugs and the cycle of the moon. In Corvallis, Oregon, Dr. N. H. Anderson, of the Department of Entomology at Oregon State University, was able to collect over 1,000 insects in specially designed trapping devices in a three-hour period when the moon was in its last quarter, but only 200 insects at the same time when the full moon was out. Other entomologists have reported that there are literally hundreds more female mosquitoes in the air during the new moon as there are during the full moon.

What this suggests, of course, is that rather than spraying ourselves with all kinds of dangerous pesticide repellents, we should plan our summer evening picnics or barbecues at times other than those on which there is going to be a new moon.

Following these scientifically controlled demonstrations of the moon's influence on various marine animals and insects, Dr. Brown began to wonder whether other, more highly developed animals are also sensitive to the cycle of the moon and he decided to investigate the phenomenon in the hamster. One reason for his choice was that the hamster is a mammal, and thus farther up the evolutionary ladder than are the marine animals. Another consideration was that there was no reason for the hamster to be sensitive to the cycle of the moon, for unlike the other animals he had studied, the moon's influence on the tides had no bearing on the life of the hamster. On the other hand, if there were a periodic lunar effect on the behavior of an animal such as the hamster, then this discovery could have important theoretical and practical value. If true for the hamster, then why not monkeys? Why not man himself? And if indeed such a lunar influence were to be discovered, then recognition of this

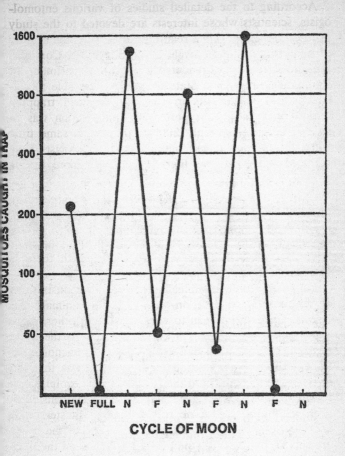

Relation between Lunar Cycle and mosquitoes in the air. More mosquitoes are lured into a "trap" during the New Moon than during the Full Moon, demonstrating more mosquitoes fly about at this time (From Hors Fall, 1943)

influence could go a long way toward accounting for, predicting, and finally controlling much of the biological uncertainty with which science and medicine must constantly contend.

To investigate the phenomenon insofar as the hamster was concerned, Dr. Brown took advantage of a general characteristic of these animals and indeed of all rodents, namely, that they tend to exhibit a regular circadian rhythm in their locomotor activity. This activity pattern can be demonstrated in the laboratory by placing these animals in cages which are attached to running wheels by means of a tunnel. Thus, whenever the hamster feels like running, all it has to do is go through the tunnel and he is free to run in the wheel to its heart's content. The wheel itself can be connected to a counter and a clocking device and the number of revolutions it undergoes at each hour of the day can be automatically determined.

With this basic apparatus, Dr. Brown kept records of the hourly rhythm of hamsters for over two years. At the end of this period he analyzed the results. Sure enough, he found that the hamster became especially active around the full moon and the new moon! Furthermore, the highest daily values occurred on exactly the same day in the moon's cycle for the two years in which the records were kept. Such regularity was undoubtedly due to some effect of the moon which was being sensed by the hamsters!

Additional experiments of the same sort were then conducted with mice and rats. Again Dr. Brown found a flurry of animation around the time of the full moon. These results suggested that mammals such as the hamster, the rat, and the mouse possess some mysterious sensitivity to the moon and that according to its position, these rodents would become overly active on certain days of the month. Somehow the moon was exciting these creatures and this excitement was being translated into increases in running. Was this the animal counterpart to the agitation in human behavior that scientists had

reported many centuries before but which had long since
been dismissed as superstition? Dr. Brown cautiously
avoided any reference to such parallels between his animal
experiments and these so-called superstitions. But the
parallel was intriguing, and it was not long before curiosity
began to be aroused about the possibility that these and
other superstitions concerning the moon might be true
after all.

IN 1492, Christopher Columbus embarked upon his great historic voyage from Spain to find a northwest passage to the spice-rich lands of far-off China. With three tiny ships, the *Nina,* the *Pinta,* and the *Santa Maria,* and no map to guide him, he set out from the Old World and discovered not the great Khan of Marco Polo's China, but the proud bronze Indians of the New World.

During the course of that eventful voyage, an interesting and puzzling event took place which baffled Columbus and his crew and which historians have been unable to explain until only quite recently.

Columbus had just sighted an island a few days before and his men wanted to land, take on water, and return to their homeland. They were understandably nervous and they were becoming more and more frightened at the unknown dangers that lurked beyond. But instead of turning back, Columbus insisted on continuing westward. Then, on the night of October 11, around 10:00 P.M., a mysterious light appeared in the distance in the middle of the sea. What could it be, he wondered? Who could be signaling them from the unknown? From the poop of the *Santa Maria,* Columbus tried to make out what it was that seemed to beckon him on, confirming his faith that land was not far beyond. But the light lasted for only a few minutes and was not seen again.

In his journal, Columbus wrote that the light appeared like "the flame of a small candle alternately raised and lowered." Although he and all the members of his crew were certain that someone or something had been signaling them, they could find no proof of any light source in the distance. The object, whatever it was, was gone as soon as it had suddenly appeared. Had there really been something out there in the sea, or were their eyes playing tricks on them all?

Samuel Eliot Morison, an expert on Columbus, states that the light was merely an hallucination: "Volumes have been written to explain what this light was or might have been," he informs us. "To a seaman it requires no explanation. It is an illusion, created by tense watchfulness. When uncertain of your exact position, and straining to make a night landfall, you are apt to see imaginary lights and flashes and to hear nonexistent bells and breakers."

This was the easy way out. If you can't explain something, something that is seen not by one or two people, but a whole crew on three different ships from three different angles, don't spend any time worrying about it, just ignore it.

Had Morison been a visitor to the islands of the Bahamas near which Columbus observed the mysterious light, and had he been familiar with the breeding habits of a tiny marine animal that lived in that area, he may have been more circumspect in his opinion.

One such visitor whose stay in the Bahamas did alert him to a more scientific explanation of the puzzling light in the sea was Dr. L. R. Crawshay, a young marine biologist at the Plymouth Laboratory of the Biological Association of the United Kingdom. One day as he was daydreaming of the Bahamas where he had just finished

working for the government, he called to mind the fasci-
nating splendor of the Atlantic fireworms during their
chaotic breeding encounter which occurred unerringly
one hour before moonrise, just before the moon's last
quarter.

The Atlantic fireworm (*Odontosyllis enopla*) is aptly
named, since the females of the species give off a brilliant
phosphorescent glow at various intervals as they beckon
male fireworms to come and mate with them. This glow
is visible not only to the enchanted observers who line
the beaches at such times, but is also discernible to sailors
from their ships. When a male and female finally come
together, the two creatures actually burst, and their sperm
and eggs are flung into the sea. The event lasts only a
few minutes and then the fireworms disappear until the
next month shortly before the moon's third quarter. What
a sight to behold, Crawshay thought to himself.

Then suddenly Crawshay recalled something from the
back of his mind about a mysterious light seen by Columbus. Could it have been the fireworms in their fertility
rites? Charged with excitement, the scientist ran to con-
sult some old almanacs. What phase was the moon in
on October 11, 1492? Crawshay had difficulty believing
what he saw. But there it was—on October 11, 1492, the
moon had one day more to go before it entered into its
last quarter!

Elated by this solution to a centuries-old enigma, Crawshay published his discovery in *Nature*, giving it the im-
posing title, "Possible Bearing of a Luminous Syllid on
the Question of the Landfall of Columbus."

The Atlantic fireworm is not the only creature in the
animal world whose fertility rites are dictated by the
cycle of the moon. One such animal that has been de-
lighting children and adults alike on the west coast of
the United States for a great many years is the California
grunion (*Leuresthes tenuis*).

The grunion is a small slender fish, five to six inches

in length, with a bluish-green back and silvery sides and belly. Like the Atlantic fireworm, it too is responsive to the movements of the moon, which in some as yet unfathomable way causes it to breed only during the three to four nights after the full or new moon in the months of February through September. At such times, thousands upon thousands of grunions make their perilous journey toward the beaches of southern California and northern Baja California for the sole purpose of creating new grunions.

The spawning run typically begins with the appearance of a few males that ride the waves onto the beach and then ride them back into the sea. About twenty minutes later the females make their appearance as they swim onto the beach, coming completely out of the water to lay their eggs in the moist sand. Once she has ventured as far onto the dry land as she dares go, the female grunion drills herself into the sand by violently wriggling her tail back and forth until she has almost buried herself. Once this has happened, her male escorts, who have accompanied her onto the dry beach, begin to wrap themselves around her body. This embrace causes the female to lay her eggs a few inches below the surface of the sand. The males now discharge their sperm onto the female. The sperm seeps down her body and onto the eggs, thus fertilizing them. Exhausted by their ordeal, the males and females now frantically make their way down the beach, hoping to catch a wave lest they be stranded and die.

For their part, the eggs remain buried in the sand and are rarely disturbed by the sea because they have been laid when the tide was highest. (As the tide ebbs, the waves are no longer able to reach the nests. The waves of succeeding tides will also be unable to reach them, since the tide is highest during the full moon, and as the moon continues on in its cycle, the tides do not reach as far up the beach. The eggs thus remain covered until the new moon, when the tides are high once again.)

In the meantime the eggs do not remain dormant. Those which were fortunate enough to have been fertilized now have tiny grunions growing in them. And only a fortnight from the time that they were conceived, these fishlets will be ready to enter the sea. Then it will only be necessary for the high tide of the new moon to wash away the sand that covers the eggs. Besides washing the sand away, the water's cold touch also serves to break open the shell. This releases the grunions, and they now try to make their way to the sea in the receding waves.

Since this spawning cycle occurs both at the time of the new and full moon, light intensity cannot account for this cyclic behavior. If tidal rhythm were the causal factor, the question then arises as to how the grunion knows that the tide has passed its maximum.

Even more spectacular, perhaps, is the breeding act of the palolo worm (*Eunice viridis*), which inhabits the rocks and coral of the South Pacific. The palolo worm is several inches in length. The male is light brown or ocher in color and the females are green and grayish indigo.

These small creatures spend their whole lives on the bottom of the sea except for two periods, which always occur seven to nine days before the full moon in the months of October and November. At these two times, and these times only, millions upon millions of these worms literally break in two. Half of each animal, the part containing the sexual organs, then rises to the surface, while the other half remains in its burrow, where it generates its missing parts. On the surface, the sea looks like a soup, a brown-and-green palolo-worm soup. Not very much later the soup takes on a milky color as the male and female organs discharge their sperm and eggs into the sea.

The natives of the South Pacific eagerly look forward to this event, for to them the palolo worm is a great

delicacy. When the great day arrives, they go out in the
sea with buckets, scooping up as many of the tiny animals
as they can, for they know that this delicacy will not be
available for another whole year.

There is also a relative of this creature of the South
Pacific, called the Atlantic palolo, whose breeding habits
are very similar. Near the Tortugos, they appear in abun-
dance around the moon's last quarter during the months
of June and July. Once again the ritual involves a splitting
of the worm's body and the appearance of countless
millions of sex organs discharging their products into the
sea.

The same event is repeated in the Malay archipelago,
where the wawo worm breeds on the second and third
nights after the full moon in March and April. Near
Japan, the bachi palolo goes through the ritual immediately after the full and new moons in October and
November. At such times, the Japanese fishermen set out
to sea to catch as many as they can, for they have found
that these worms are an excellent and easily obtainable
bait.

At one time it was suggested that the cause of these
curious phenomena was the movement of the tides. However, this argument has convincingly been disproved,
since at the full moon these worms breed naturally in
tanks of water where there are no tides to stimulate them.

Furthermore, at the University of Freiburg, in Germany,
scientists have been studying another worm, *Platynereis
dumerilii*, which rises to the surface of the sea to breed
around the last quarter of the moon. The scientists kept
some of these worms in tanks of water and exposed them
to constant light conditions to see if the worm would still
maintain its breeding cycle. Under such conditions, the
rhythm was completely lost. However, if in addition to
the constant bright light, another bright light was introduced into the laboratory for only two nights in the
month, the worms responded to it as if it were the full

moon and began to breed exactly one week later, that is, at a time equivalent to the last quarter of the moon. The scientists also found that if the worms were not ready to breed at that time, they would postpone their sexual rendezvous for thirty-five days, at a date when the moon would be in its third quarter in the next month.

These observations indicate that even if the moon were covered by clouds for nearly the whole of the month, it would only require two cloudless nights for the male and female worms to be able to synchronize their breeding cycles so as to come together in the sea. And even should the clouds obscure the moon every night of the month the worms could still keep their appointments at the surface of the sea, because in some unknown way, they are able to recall the time of the full moon in the previous month.

Whatever the basis for this relationship between the moon and the breeding cycle of these marine animals, the synchrony of the reproductive activity with the phases of the moon is of enormous biological importance for the sheer survival of these creatures. Were it not for the fact that the moon stimulated the males and females to reach their sexual peaks at exactly the same time, their sperm and eggs would never come in contact, owing to the vastness of the sea. By spawning at a specific time and place, however, the eggs tend to remain relatively concentrated in a particular area long enough so that their chances of being fertilized are greatly increased. As a result, the species is perpetuated.

Many centuries ago, the Greek philosopher Aristotle observed that the ova in sea urchins also increase in size in synchrony with the cycle of the moon. This observation has long since been corroborated by experiments which do indeed indicate that the gonads of the sea urchin grow to become engorged before the full moon, when spawning occurs. After spawning and the evacuation of the gonads, the cycle repeats itself, and the empty gonads

fill up once more as they wait to be emptied again at the
next full moon. The sea scallop is another marine animal
that has been observed to have its greatest frequency of
spawning at the time of the full moon and its minimum
during the new moon

Although these lunar-dependent reproductive cycles are
of interest in themselves, they also pose important eco-
nomic considerations for those in the fishing industry.
For instance, in northeastern New Zealand, commercial
fishermen tend to work much harder and longer during
certain phases of the moon because it has been their experience that fish in that area are more abundant and
more easily caught during those times. Elsewhere in that
part of the world, other fishermen have found that clean-
ing the hulls of their ships is best done at times other
than around the new or full moon, since at these times,
insect larvae tend to attach themselves to the hulls more
often than at other times in the moon's cycle. Consequently, if the hulls are cleaned at other times, they tend
to remain unfouled for a longer period.

Because of its biological significance, it would be surprising if this relationship between the moon and reproductive cycles did not occur in land animals as well, and
in fact this has been shown to be the case.

Adult mayflies, for example, have an active life span
that is measured in hours, rather than days or weeks.
For most of their life they remain dormant, but in the
month of May they emerge from their sleep for the sole
purpose of finding a mate in order to breed and hence
perpetuate their species. In the temperate climates of the
earth, the breeding act is triggered by the light and temperature conditions in May, but in tropical countries, the
climate changes very minimally from month to month.
As a result, the time for sexual rendezvous must be
triggered by some other cue. In Africa, around Lake
Victoria, scientists have now discovered that the stimulus
which summons the mayflies to their breeding duties in

that part of the world is none other than the majesty of the full moon.

Nor are these lunar-dependent reproductive rhythms confined to primitive organisms. Detailed studies of the reproductive cycle of the Malayan forest rat, conducted by Dr. J. L. Harrison, have now confirmed the fact that the greatest number of conceptions in these animals take place around the time of the full moon. According to Dr. O. Ramanathan, the Indian buffalo exhibits a lunar-dependent cycle in its breeding habits as well.

At Yale University, Dr U. Cowgill and her associates have also detected an increase in sexual behavior in a number of primates, our evolutionary ancestors, which coincides with the cycle of the moon. After carefully examining their records, they state that their findings "appear to suggest a *prima facie* case for a correlation between peaks of sexual activity and the lunar cycle in the two primate species *Lemur spp.* and *Galago spp.*"

Dr. Cowgill's studies also tend to corroborate the observations of a Dutch army physician named Hill, who noted that guenon monkeys in Surinam, South America, near the equator, exhibited "an abundant sanguinous flow occurring at every new moon and lasting about three days, the animal at this time showing signs of sexual excitement." Dr. Hill's observation and other related comments can be found in *The Psychology of Sex*, the encyclopedic work by the pioneer sexologist Havelock Ellis.

Although usually conservative in his scientific generalizations, Charles Darwin, whose theories of evolution changed man's concept of himself and made him aware that he had more in common with the other animals of the world than he cared to admit, expressed himself in this manner concerning the moon's possible influence on mankind: "Man is subject, like other mammals, birds and even insects," he stated, "to that mysterious law, which causes certain normal processes, such as gestation, as well as the maturation and duration of various diseases, to follow lunar periods."

It was thus apparent to Darwin that like many animals, man was also subject to the mysterious power of the moon.

It has also long been thought that the human female's desire for sex is highest around the time she ovulates, but a detailed investigation of this belief has only recently been conducted. In this study, thirty women who were not taking birth-control pills were enlisted as volunteers, and they each agreed to discuss their sexual feelings and to keep a record of their menstrual cycle for a total of seventy-five cycles. The data were then analyzed and the feelings of these women regarding sex were carefully compared with their menstrual cycles. The analysis indicated that there was a clear increase in the female libido around the time of ovulation.

This in itself did not implicate the moon. But a few additional facts seemed to point in that direction. It is now known, for example, that the female menstrual cycle, which we shall discuss in detail in the next chapter, does not average twenty-eight days, although this is still taught in many textbooks, but rather averages 29.5 days, coinciding exactly with the synodic-lunar monthly cycle. Further study has also shown that the average human gestation period—that is, the time between the day of conception and the day of birth—is exactly nine lunar month ($29.5 \times 9 = 265.5$ days). Thus, by counting backwards from the day of birth, it is possible to pinpoint the day of conception, and this time can then be related to the position of the moon. As we shall see momentarily, a significant number of women ovulate around the time of the full moon. If this is also the time at which their libidos are highest, when they are more likely to desire sexual union. They are also more likely to conceive. It is to this relationship between the moon, the menstrual cycle, and the birth rate that we now turn our attention.

FROM time immemorial, the belief in a peculiarly unique connection between women and the moon has existed. In ancient Babylon, for example, fertility, pregnancy, and birth were all deemed to be under the influence of the moon. Those women whose lives had been singulary consecrated to the moon cult therefore were looked upon as being impregnated by the moon, and their children were called "children of the moon." In ancient Persia, the moon was hailed as the god who was "rich in seed, in milk, in fat, in marrow, and in offspring." In ancient Egypt, the Temple of the Moon at Thebes bore an inscription which stated, "Through his [the moon's] gazing women conceive."

At back of this hoary belief in the moon's influence on fertility was the observation that the time between the human menstrual cycle and the time of the lunar cycle were quite similar in duration. This in turn led to the inference that the moon was actually responsible for the female cycle. Such a relationship between the moon and the menses, in fact, is still accepted as factual by many primitive tribal societies and has ever entered our own language in terms such as "catamenia," which is derived from the Greek words *kata* and *men*, meaning "by the moon." This relationship between the menstrual and lunar cycles is also evident in many other languages as well. The French, for example, refer to the menstrual cycle as *le moment de la lune*, "the moment of the moon," whereas in Germany, many of the countryfolk still refer to menstruation as "the moon." In New Zealand, the Maiori refer to menstruation as *mata marama* which roughly means "moon sickness," and they believe that a young girl's first menstruation is a consequence of the moon's union with her while she is asleep.

The ancient Hindus likewise believed that menstruation was proof that females were subject to the moon's influence, and this belief was formulated into a simple precept which was incorporated into the Veda, their holy scripture. According to the text, "the blood of the woman is a form of Agni and therefore no one should despise it," Agni being the word for fire, which to them was closely related to the light of the moon.

Our own word "sabbath" is derived from the Babylonian word *sabattu*, which also has its roots in the relationship between the moon and menstruation. According to the Babylonians, Ishtar, the moon goddess, was considered to be menstruating when the moon was full, and this *sabattu*, or evil day, was regarded as inopportune for work, for preparing food, or for doing anything except resting. The Jewish idea of the sabbath is closely, if not directly, related to the Babylonian *sabattu*, and it is interesting to note that the Jews came to Palestine from the area around Babylon. From the Jews, the idea of the sabbath passed directly into Christianity, and although this day of observance is no longer connected with the ancient belief of the Babylonians, their ideas about the moon and menstruation and the taboos associated with the latter are mainly responsible for our own idea that the sabbath should be a day of rest.

For their part, the ancient Greeks were not only convinced that the menstrual cycle was governed by the course of the moon, they even went so far as to account for the relationship. "The commencement of the menses in women occurs at a time when the moon is waning," Aristotle wrote. "On this account, certain men who pretend to know, assert that the moon is feminine since the monthly period in women coincides with the waning of the moon, and after the wane and discharge, both grow whole again."

Aristotle then went on to give what he considered a reasonable explanation for the phenomenon: "To consider now the region of the uterus in the female, the two blood vessels, the great vessel [i.e., the vena cava] and the aorta, divide higher up, and many fine vessels from them terminate in the uterus. These become overfilled with the nourishment they convey, nor is the female nature able to concoct it, because it is colder than man's; so the blood is excreted through the fine vessels into the uterus, these being unable on account of their narrowness to receive the excessive quantity, the result is a sort of hemorrhage. The period is not accurately defined in women, but tends to return during the waning of the moon. This we should expect, for the bodies of animals are colder when the environment happens to become so, and the time of the change from one month to another is cold because of the absence of the moon."

Apparently Aristotle held the opinion that the moon produced a certain warmth when it was at its fullest but that as it waned, its power to give off heat diminished. This in turn caused animals, and particularly women, to become colder. As a result, Aristotle believed they became unable to retain their full reservoir of blood and so were caused to lose some of that blood via the menses.

In many primitive societies, the mentrual flow is still often attributed to the moon's influence, and in some instances, the nature of that influence is thought to be the result of direct sexual intercourse between the moon and the menstruating woman. In the Murray Islands, for instance, some tribes believe that the moon assumes the shape of a young man and in this form has intercourse with women. In the upper Amazon, the Uaupe Indians actually refer to a girl's first menstrual flow as the "defloration by the moon."

In addition to causing menstruation, the moon was also held to be responsible for conception, and this is still believed to be the case in many primitive societies. The Maiori of New Zealand, hold that the moon is the father of all children. The Eskimos are convinced that the moon comes down from the heavens and actually ravishes their women. This idea can also be traced back to very ancient times. For instance, in the hoary religious texts of the Hindus, it is written that the moon god, Soma, is physically responsible for impregnating women. This belief is also clearly stated by the Roman orator Cicero. "The moon," he states, "is the source of conception and birth and of growth and maturity."

So ingrained are these beliefs that in many primitive tribes, women are often held blameless for any children that they may conceive. Instead, it is the moon that is held directly accountable. This in turn implies that sexual intercourse between men and women will have no effect on the female's conceiving, and therefore, it is not uncommon to find a fair amount of sexual promiscuity in many of those tribes that entertain such opinions. It is also for this reason that the incidences of promiscuity increase during particular phases of the moon. Among the Bantu of South Australia, for example, the coming of the full moon is the signal for sexual abandon. In British Columbia, Canada, the chiefs of the Nutka Indians made a special point of having intercourse with their wives in the presence of the full moon if they wished children. In Scotland, the belief in the moon's influence on fertility at one time contributed to the unwillingness of many a young lass to become bethrothed except during the time of the full moon.

The actual time of birth, as all astrologers are wont to teach, is thought to be especially influential as far as strength of body is concerned. This belief is, however, not peculiar to astrology, since many writers who either knew nothing of divination or else scoffed at such activity wrote of the moon's influence in this regard. For example, in the ancient treatise *On Animals*, Aelian states matter-of-factly that "young beasts of burden that are born when the moon is on the wane are less capable and feebler than others, and what is more, knowledge of these matters recommend that animals born in this part of the month should not be reared on the ground that they are not of good quality."

Although no defender of astrological doctrine, Francis Bacon in his *Natural History* voiced identical beliefs: "It may be that children and young cattle that are brought forth in the full of the moon, are stronger and larger than those brought forth in the wane." Similarly, the nineteenth-century French physician La Martinière states: "I have noticed that this planet [the moon] has such enormous power over living creatures, that children born at the first quarter of the declining moon [i.e., the third quarter, when the moon is on the wane], are more subject to illness, so that children born when there is no moon [*i.e.*, the time of the new moon], if they live, are weaker, delicate, and sickly, or are of little mind or idiots."

So much for the beliefs of the past. We have no way of knowing for certain how such ideas originated, but their persistence over time and space is intriguing and has prompted more than a few scientists to investigate whether or not there actually is any relationship between the lunar cycle and female sexuality.

It is now known that menstruation occurs as a result of the actions of a number of hormones which are produced by the pituitary gland. This tiny gland is located in the head very near the brain, and it sends out hormones which are actually chemical messengers that circulate through the blood and cause the female ovary to release an egg (ovum) into the reproductive tract.

Today we know that the female menstrual cycle occurs as a result of changes that take place in the uterus as it prepares to receive a potential embryo. What happens is that the blood vessels in the uterus begin to increase in anticipation of a fertilized egg implanting itself. The egg, or ovum as it is sometimes called, is released from the ovary at the time of ovulation and lives for only about forty-eight hours unless it is fertilized by a sperm. If fertilization of the female ovum does not take place, there is no embryo and the unfertilized ovum is expelled, the blood vessels in the uterus rupture, and the menstrual bleeding period begins.

While scientists now comprehend the physiological processes involved in menstruation, they are still at a loss to explain the curious correlation that has often been observed between the female menstrual period in a great many women and the moon's cycle as it passes around the earth.

One of the first modern investigations of this relationship between the lunar and female cycle was conducted in 1898 by the Nobel Prize–winning Danish scientist, Svante Arrhenius. Arrhenius carefully charted the cycles of over 12,000 women in a Stockholm maternity hospital and compared these with the position of the moon. The close relationship in time between the two convinced him that the moon did indeed have some special effect on the female menstrual cycle.

In 1936, two German physicians, Guthmann and Oswald, reported that of the 10,000 women they studied, more of them had their periods at the time of the full or new moon than at any other time in the moon's cycle.

A quarter of a century later, in 1962, an eminent

Czechoslovakian scientist, Dr. Jeri Malek, addressed a meeting of scientists at the New York Academy of Sciences, on factors affecting menstruation. One of the factors influencing the female menstrual period, he said, was the position of the moon. Of the 7,420 women whose menstrual cycles he had been closely following over a long period of time, Malek reported that the onset of bleeding had been noted as taking place more often around the time of the full moon than during any other time of the month.

Although Dr. Malek was unable to explain just how the moon influenced the female reproductive system, numerous authors have frequently pointed out the interesting observation that a large percentage of women exhibit the same reproductive responsiveness to the lunar cycle as do many of the marine animals we mentioned earlier. Is it possible that this similarity reflects some kind of evolutionary inheritance?

Charles Darwin, the originator of the theory of evolution, thought so. In the *Descent of Man*, a book which he wrote in 1871, Darwin pointed to the coincidence between the reproductive cycles of the human female and that of marine animals as proof that evolution had occurred from the more primitive creatures of the sea. "Man is descended from fish," Darwin declared, and therefore, "why should not the 28-day feminine cycle be a vestige of the past when life depended on the tides, and therefore the moon."

Although Darwin felt that the moon brought on the reproductive cycle in marine animals via its influence on the tides, studies conducted after his death, many of which have been referred to above, have demonstrated that this effect on the reproductive cycle is not due to the tides but instead is a more direct result of the moon's influence on living things.

One possibility that may account for the moon's influence on reproductive cycles in animals and human females arises from an interesting discovery originally reported by Dr. Harold Burr of Yale University.

During the course of some studies with plants and animals, Dr. Burr found that the electrical potential or voltage that is characteristic of all living matter, undergoes a definite pattern of cyclic variation. At some times, the electrical potential of plants, animals, and the human body is very high. At other times it is relatively low. After studying this peculiar phenomenon for many years, Dr. Burr found that a relatively large increase in electrical potential in the female body occurs once a month and lasts for about twenty-four hours. Furthermore, this increase appears to occur between menstrual cycles, and Dr. Burr thought it might in some way be connected with ovulation, the release of eggs from the female ovary.

This idea was subsequently proved to be correct during an operation on a female patient who agreed to participate in one of Dr. Burr's experiments. Dr. Burr had been testing this woman daily for several days while she was in the hospital waiting to undergo surgery. Since the operation was of a minor nature and did not necessitate immediate concern, Dr. Burr was able to continue watching for any changes in her electrical potential without any danger to her welfare.

At last, on the day that Burr's instruments indicated that the woman's electrical potential had markedly increased, she was sent to surgery. During the operation, which involved examination of her ovaries, the doctors found that she had indeed just ovulated on that very day, just as Burr had predicted on the basis of the changes in her body's electrical potential.

The next clue to the moon's influence on the female menstrual cycle comes from a report by Dr. Leonard Ravitz, a physician at Duke University in Durham, North Carolina. Dr. Ravitz was also interested in the changes in electrical potential that take place in the body, and during the course of his studies, he found that these changes in electrical potential increase maximally during the full moon in many women.

Here, then, was a possible basis for the cosmic connection between the moon and the female reproductive cycle. When full, the moon causes a dramatic increase in the electric potential of the female body. This change in turn triggers the release of an egg from the ovaries. If unfertilized, the ovum is expelled from the body, and menstrual bleeding occurs. If fertilized, a child is conceived. We will see momentarily that not only is there an influence of the moon on the time of the month when a woman menstruates, but the time of birth is also controlled to a great extent by the moon.

This relationship between the moon and conception was actually put to the test on a rather large scale not so long ago, by a freak accident that occurred on November, 9, 1965, which has otherwise become known as "Black Tuesday."

Those Americans living on the east coast of the United States at that time will remember that on the night of November 9, there was a great power failure and the entire eastern seaboard was plunged into complete darkness. There was no electric light, no television, no radio. Elevators were stuck between floors. Food thawed in the refrigerators. It was a night of seeming chaos.

Eventually the power was restored, and the event was soon forgotten. Or so it seemed. But nine months later, there was a sudden increase in the number of babies appearing in the hospitals of the northeastern United States.

The newspapers noted the occurrence of the "baby boom" and pointed out that the scientists must all be wrong; it was not light but darkness that stimulated mating activity.

There was another explanation that they failed to consider, however, one that they would hardly have missed had they taken the time to look up their almanacs or inspected photographs that they had taken of that night, nine months before. "Black Tuesday," they should have remembered, was a night in which there was a full silvery moon in the skies overlooking the earth.

6.   The Moon and the Maternity Ward

NOT only does the moon affect the female menstrual cycle, it is also thought to determine the date of childbirth.

Perhaps this belief owes its origins to the similarities in shape between the developing pregnant woman and the moon as it goes through its cycle. The waxing moon increasing in size to a full rounded orb and then growing smaller and smaller until it was nothing more than a sliver of light was reminiscent of the growing stomach of the pregnant woman and its subsequent decrease after the birth of her child.

A second factor influencing the belief of the moon's influence over birth was the already existing veneration of the moon as the fertilizing energy force, the force that makes plants and animals grow and thrive. As the fructifying force in nature, the moon assumed a position of prime importance in conception and birth in the primitive mind. These beliefs gained substance from observations over long centuries of time that more babies came into the world when the moon was full than at any other time of the month. Thus, the ideas and the facts all seemed to come together for our ancestors.

Recently I attended a series of lectures given by the head nurse of the obstetrical wing of a large hospital, on prenatal and postnatal care of infants. Most of the people in the audience were soon-to-be mothers and fathers. One of the lectures given by the nurse was dedicated to the various superstitions associated with pregnancy and birth. The nurse covered all the old wives' tales about children in great detail, since from past experience, she had found that questions about these superstitions were always asked at the end of her lectures, no matter how silly they seemed. The nurse mentioned the popular misguided idea that babies born with birthmarks resembling animals or objects had had these imprinted on their bodies when their mothers became frightened by these things during pregnancy. Another old myth was the one that an expectant mother should avoid looking at deformed people because the sight of their disfigurement might cause their own children to become deformed.

After the lecture, the nurse invited questions from the audience, and a very soon-to-be mother raised her hand and asked in a rather nervous voice why the superstition about more children being born during the full and new moons had not been mentioned.

"Because," replied the nurse, "that is not a superstition. It is a fact."

The room suddenly grew quiet as the nurse explained that in the hospital she had been working in for quite some time now, experience had taught her and the other nurses on the obstetrics ward to expect a busy night in the delivery room when the moon was full.

Although the belief in a lunar influence on birth rate has been considered nothing more than a bit of antiquated folklore by most doctors, the nurse explained that as a rule, doctors were in the hospital for only a few hours each day. They delivered one or two babies each, and then they went back to their offices. The nurses, however, remained on the maternity ward sometimes as long as sixteen hours a day. They knew the days to look out for because they spent more hours out of that long day helping mothers to deliver. And they worked with all the doctors. They saw more births than the doctors, and their tired feet told them when they had had a particularly busy day.

Not all obstetricians, however, disagree with the observations of this head nurse. In fact, over the years a considerable body of scientific evidence has begun to accumulate from all over the world, showing that the birth rate unquestionably increases around the time of the full and new moon.

For example, in 1929, the prestigious French medical journal *La Presse Medicale* reported that just after the full moon, the birth rate was more than double what it was during any other phase of the lunar cycle.

In 1938, Dr. H. Gunther of the city of Cologne, Germany, reported a similar finding concerning the increase in the birth rate around the full and new moon.

In the prelude to his own study of this curious relationship between the moon and childbirth, Dr. A. G. Schnurman, an obstetrician practicing in Roanoke, Virginia, corroborated the impression of nurses throughout the country that the moon influences the time of birth. "I have often heard the nurses in the obstetrical service state," Schnurman says, "that the moon has changed and we will be getting a new bunch of O.B.'s."

His curiosity piqued, Schnurman decided to study the matter for himself. Since the Roanoke hospital maintained detailed records of when each baby in that hospital was born, Schnurman looked back over the past files of the hospital and tabulated the day on which each child had been born for the last five years. After examining all these birth records, Schnurman found that in forty out of sixty months, or in 66.7 percent of the months studied, the greatest number of births unquestionably had taken place around the time of the full moon or twenty-four hours just before or after!

"Just what all this means I am incapable of stating," Schnurman concluded, but he did venture one possible explanation based on an inappropriate analogy with the moon's influence on the tides. "One may theorize," he suggests, "that there is a lunar effect possibly electronic on the amniotic fluid as a body of water just as on the tides of water elsewhere."

In 1959, Dr. Walter Menaker caused a considerable stir in the medical profession when he corroborated Dr. Schnurman's findings. According to the results of his analysis of over a half-million births in the city of New York between January 1948 and January 1957, the highest frequency of deliveries throughout the city occurred around the time of the full moon. The findings of this study, which appeared in the *American Journal of Obstetrics and Gynecology*, generated a great deal of interest on the part of obstetricians throughout the country. No longer could the medical profession smile at the seeming naivety of bygone centuries. The folk wisdom they had previously dismissed out of hand was now proving to be true.

In the same year that Dr. Menaker reported his study, Dr. Edson J. Andrews was causing his medical colleagues to sit up and take notice when he reported his own findings concerning the relationship between the lunar cycle and the birth rate, at a meeting of physicians in Miami, Florida.

Dr. Andrews was amazed when he plotted the frequency of births at the Tallahassee Memorial Hospital for the years 1956, 1957, and 1958 against the phases of the moon. Four hundred and one babies had been born within two days of the full moon, 375 had been born within two days of the new moon, and only 320 had been born within two days of the moon's first quarter!

In 1967, Dr. Menaker reported his analysis of a further

half-million births in New York City covering the period from January 1961 to December 1963. Once again, he found that the highest frequency of births occurred around the time of the full moon.

In 1973, another analysis of the birth records from New York City was reported, this time by Dr. M. Osley of the State University of New York at Buffalo. Over a three-year period involving a half-million births, Osley found a significant increase in the number of births occurring just before the full moon. The number of births occurring at the exact time of the full moon was also found to be above average.

As a consequence of these various studies indicating a definite relationship between birth rate and the lunar cycle, Dr. Menaker has suggested that one practical application of these findings is that in cases where a couple wish to have a child, the most favorable time for sexual relations would appear to be just before the full moon. This idea arises from the fact that the normal gestation period for a baby is forty weeks, or ten lunar months, and further corroborates the moon's ability to influence the release of eggs from the female ovary, which we discussed in the previous chapter. Conversely, if a couple wished to minimize the chances of conception, they would be advised to refrain from sexual relations when the moon is full.

These observations have now been carried one step further by Dr. Eugene Jonas, Director of the Psychiatric Department of one of the State Clinics in Czechoslovakia. In working with a number of female patients, Dr. Jonas observed that a great many of them exhibited a periodic increase in sexuality. At first, Dr. Jonas was at a loss to explain this behavior, but eventually his research efforts forced him to conclude that sexuality and indeed the chances of a woman conceiving a child at all were greatest during the same phase of the moon as was present when she herself was born.

Moreover, he also found that he could successfully predict the sex of the child by determining the position of the moon on the day of conception! "At first," writes Dr. Jonas, "I regarded these things as fantastic and I could not bring myself to believe in their truth. However, my observations and examinations, running into thousands of cases in the gynecological clinic in Pozzony [Bratislava, Czechoslovakia], showed me that the more obstetric cases I studied and the more exact the astronomical calculations I carried out, the more did the results show the existence of the hitherto unknown law of nature."

Astounding as this may seem, Dr. Jonas' findings have been put to the test in various European countries and have been corroborated by independent groups of gynecologists. In 1960, at the meeting of the Second Clinic of Gynecology, held in Bratislava, a number of impartial physicians reported confirmation of his findings. In 1964, Dr. Jonas presented his findings to the Czechoslovak Academy of Sciences' Conference on Bio-rhythm. "We can't ignore the statements of Dr. Jonas," admitted Dr. J. Malek of the Prague Gynecology Clinic, whose own independent studies have also shown a lunar influence on the female menstrual cycle. In Hungary, Dr. K. Rechnitz, Associate Professor of Gynecology at the First Gynecological Clinic in Budapest, has employed Jonas' method and likewise reports that he is able to predict in advance the sex of a newborn child with an accuracy of 94 percent. In his own country, an official government-sponsored committee of gynecologists tested Dr. Jonas' ability to predict the sex of a child and found him to be 83 percent accurate. (Chance—that is, mere guessing—would only be at the 50 percent level.) Dr. Jonas' findings have also been verified by scientists at the famous Max Planck Institute in Heidelberg, Germany. In Munich, Dr. R. Tomascheck, president of the International Society of Geophysics, has now expressed open support of Dr. Jonas.

As a consequence of his discoveries, Dr. Jonas has

now established clinics in a number of European countries which will inform female patients of periods of high and low fertility. In his own country, the Ministry of Health has set up the Astra Research Center for Planned Parenthood at Nitra, Czechoslovakia, to provide similar information.*

In addition to the moon's influence on the number of births in a given period, there is also some indication from tests with animals that the position of the moon (perigee vs. apogee) may also have an effect on subsequent behavior.

The evidence comes primarily from a study reported in 1971 by Dr. M. A. Persinger, of the University of Manitoba, in Canada. Dr. Persinger's primary interest was the study of how low-frequency electromagnetic fields, such as those which occur in nature, affect the behavior of animals. Persinger already knew that such electromagnetic forces could significantly influence human reaction times and ambulatory behavior in infrahuman species, and he wondered whether these same forces might in some way also affect the adult behavior of animals born and raised in an electromagnetic field.

To explore this issue, he bred female rats so that they would give birth on specific days before or after the perigee and apogee of the moon. Half of these pregnant females were placed between two magnets rotating in opposite directions during the length of their pregnancy, while the other half were placed in an identical situation except that the magnets were absent. As soon as the baby rats were born, they and their mothers were removed from these conditions and were housed in ordinary laboratory cages. At twenty-one days of age, the young rats were then placed in an enclosed area which had been marked off in squares, and the number of squares each animal traversed in a given amount of time was recorded.

*Closed following the Russian invasion of Czechoslovakia.

According to psychological testing theory, the more squares an animal traverses in such situations (i.e., the greater the activity) the more curious and less fearful it is.

The results indicated that the position of the moon at the time of birth had no effect whatsoever on the ambulatory behavior of the control animals. However, in the case of those animals whose mothers had been placed in the electromagnetic field during their pregnancy, there was a definite effect of the moon's position. Those born at or near the perigee of the moon hardly moved at all when placed in the test apparatus. Those raised under identical conditions but born at or near the time of lunar apogee, however, traversed significantly more squares, suggesting that they were either more curious or less fearful than those born at the time of perigee. Thus, these results appear to suggest that there may be some long-term effect of the moon on subsequent behavior as well as on the time of delivery.

7. The Moon and the Growth of Plants

IN Deuteronomy, Chapter 33, Verses 13–14, we read: "Blessed of the Lord be this land . . . for the precious fruits brought forth by the Sun and for the precious things put forth by the Moon." These simple Biblical verses, written over 2,500 years ago, testify to the belief that the moon, as well as the sun, affects the growth of vegetation.

The Hebrews of the Bible were not the only ancient people to credit the moon with some mysterious power over plant life. In Babylonia, a civilization much older than the Hebrew, the moon goddess, Ishtar, was called the "Green One" and the "All-Dewey One." It was she alone, of all the gods and goddesses who ruled the earth, who was venerated as protectress of the rivers and springs which came out of the earth and gave life to plants in the hot, dry desert lands of Mesopotamia. It is not surprising, then, that temples to her divine spirit were often erected in the grottoes which dotted the desert, where a natural spring meant not only vegetation, but survival. It is also not surprising that prayers were offered to her divine spirit before seeds were planted and before crops were harvested.

Although civilizations such as the Babylonian disappeared, leaving little physical trace of their existence, the ideas which these people formulated did not die with them but were often adopted and refined by other civilizations with whom they came in contact. As a result of such contact, for instance, the Greeks began to study the ways in which the moon affected plant growth. So impressed did the Greeks become with the moon's influence over plants that they placed the moon even before the sun in terms of life-giving powers.

This admiration for the moon is well summed up in comments made in the first century A.D. by the famous historian and philosopher Plutarch, who taught his students that "the moon with her humid and generative light is favorable to the propagation of animals and plants, while the sun with his fierce fire scorches and burns up all growing things."

Experiments that we shall cite momentarily have proved that there is in fact more rainfall around the time of the full moon and that seeds absorb more moisture during the full moon than at any other time of the month. Therefore, if seeds are to receive the life-giving moisture they need to germinate and thrive, what better time to sow than at a time when rain is most probable?

The Romans were also convinced that the moon influenced rainfall and the moisture content of the air. Pliny, a famous naturalist of the first century A.D., told his readers that the moon was the planet of breath "because it saturates the earth [with water] and by its approach [*i.e.*, as the moon becomes full] fills bodies, while by its departure it empties them."

It was not until the sixteenth century, however, that the first actual experiments were conducted to test the ancient precepts concerning the moon's influence on plant growth. The pioneer experimenter was a scientist of world renown, Sir Francis Bacon, who is credited with advancing what is presently known as "the scientific method."

Bacon's great contribution to science was the set of guidelines he established for conducting scientific experimentation such that experiments reported by one scientist could be redone by others by following the steps he had outlined. In this way, one scientist could check on another. Another important innovation introduced by Bacon into scientific methodology was the concept of the "control" group. It was not enough to demonstrate that X caused Y to happen; Bacon said that a scientist also had to show that when everything else remained the same except for X, Y no longer happened.

In one of his famous experiments, Bacon outlined the procedure he had used to demonstrate that the moon did indeed affect the growth of plants. The following directives are his instructions to others who might wish to do the experiment themselves:

"Take some seeds, or roots [like onions, etc.], and set some of them immediately after the change [the new moon], and others of the same kind immediately after the full. Let them be as like as can be, the earth also the same as near as may be; therefore best in pots. Let the pots also stand where no rain or sun may come to them, lest the difference of weather confound the experiment. Then see in what time the seeds set on the increase of the moon came to a certain height; and how they differ from those that are set in the decrease of the moon."

According to J. G. Frazier, whose ten-volume work *The Golden Bough* is still a standard reference in the field of anthropology, planting by the moon is still a widespread custom among primitive peoples throughout the world. Brazilian tribesmen, for instance, believe that all vegetables are created by the moon and in observance of this belief they call it the "mother of plants," and they sow and harvest according to its particular phases. In central Africa, a unique ceremony is connected with this belief in the moon's generative powers: The king's placenta, which has been dutifully preserved, is left out in the open immediately after the time of the new moon. Frazier conjectures that the purpose of this ceremony is to invigorate the king by means of the waxing moon's influence on the placenta (which is supposed to represent a kind of external soul).

In the United States, folk customs concerning the moon's influence have been more conventional. In North Carolina, for example, farmers planted potatoes "in the old of the moon" and cabbage during the new moon "to make them head up well." In Buffalo Valley, central Pennsylvania, the Pennsylvania Germans taught their children the following agricultural precepts: "Beans planted when the horns of the moon are up will readily pole, but if planted when the horns are down will not; plant early potatoes when the horns of the moon are up, else they will go too deep in the ground; plant onions when the horns of the moon are down; all cereals, when planted in the waxing of the moon, will germinate more rapidly than if planted in the waning of the moon. The same is true of the ripening of the grain."

The Reverend Dr. Samuel Deane (1733–1814) wrote as follows concerning similar beliefs and practices in Portsmouth, Maine, in the eighteenth century: "Some may think it whimsical to gather them [apples] on the day above mentioned [the day of the full moon]. But, as we know both animals and vegetables are influenced by the moon in some cases, why may we not suppose a greater quantity of spirit is sent up into the fruit, when the attraction of the heavenly bodies is greatest? If so, I gather my apples at the time of their greatest perfection, when they have most in them that tends to their preservation—I suspect that the day of the moon's conjunction with the sun may answer as well; but I have not experience of it. The same caution, I doubt not, should be observed in gathering other fruits, and even apples for cider: But I have not proved it by experiment."

Unfortunately, we do not know the nature of the experiments Reverend Deane performed to convince himself of the validity of his beliefs. Nehemiah Grew, one of the founders of the modern science of botany, likewise was convinced that there was good evidence for the moon's influence on germination. Writing in his now classic text the *Anatomy of Plants*, Grew stated that "of all annual plants, in which there are successive generations of buds, one under another in one year . . . the successive generations of under buds begin at stated times; as in some plants, at every new moon, in others, at the full moon; and in some perhaps, with both or every fortnight."

Although our forefathers were quite convinced of the moon's influence on plant growth, a conviction that had a goodly amount of scientific support from some of the best-known scientists of the past, somewhere along the line of history, many of the truths of these agricultural precepts concerning the moon's influence on plant growth came to be rejected as the folly of ages past. Priding themselves on the advances of their own age, subsequent generations looked with disdain on what their fathers and grandfathers had had to say about the forces that controlled life and growth. Encased in their cities, modern men lost rapport with nature. As men moved from the farms to the cities, they ceased to appreciate the influence which celestial spheres such as the moon exerted on the lives of the plants that ultimately fed them.

However, in the twentieth century, many of these truths have been rediscovered. As man grew more and more sophisticated, he gained new respect for folklore: Just because some idea was old, it did not necessarily mean that it was wrong.

The first of the modern scientific studies to be conducted regarding the moon's effect on plant growth were performed by a Dr. Lily Kolisko. Working at the Biological Institute in Stuttgart, Germany, Kolisko spent ten years between 1926 and 1935 sowing the seeds of various leaf- and fruit-bearing plants such as cabbages, lettuces, beans, cucumbers, peas, and tomatoes, and root crops such as radishes, carrots, beetroots, and kohlrabi at different times during the moon's cycle. After ten years of detailed and meticulous research, Kolisko felt that she could speak with authority on the moon's influence on plant growth.

The following is a brief summary of some of her studies:

Maize. When sown two days before the full moon, the plants appeared stronger, the cobs were larger, and the leaves thicker than was the case for plants sown two days before the new moon. These differences were not as marked if the seeds were sown at exactly the time of the full or new moon. The conclusion of this experiment with maize is, writes Kolisko, that it "is a plant which needs the forces of the full moon at sowing time. Maize planted at new moon does not do well."

Lettuce, cabbage and *savoy.* Seedlings planted two days before full moon showed the more vigorous growth. Nearly all seedlings sown before the full moon germinated, whereas not all of those sown before new moon did so. At maturity, plants sown before full moon were about three times heavier and the yield was 30 to 40 percent higher than in the case of plants sown before new moon.

Tomatoes. Those sown two days before full moon appear more vigorous and have more juicy fruits than those sown before new moon. "From the experiments of many years," writes Kolisko, "we can recommend with good conscience that tomatoes should be sown two days before the full moon."

Radishes. Those sown two days before full moon appear to have better foliage and roots. The full-moon radish is mild in taste, whereas the new-moon radish is "biting."

Carrots. Full-moon carrots have a smoother surface than new-moon carrots, which appear more shriveled. The former are also juicier and have a milder and sweeter taste than the latter, which taste rather bitter and astringent.

In summary, Dr. Kolisko found that the most auspicious time for sowing seeds was two days before the full moon. When sown at this time, the mature plants were observed to grow larger and more vigorously than when sown at any other time of the month. Moreover, just the opposite effect was obtained if plants were sown two days before the new moon. Thus, the belief that crops produce larger yields if sown during the waxing moon was confirmed.

Several years after the publication of these studies, Dr. Harold S. Burr of Yale University, whom we mentioned earlier in connection with his work on electrical potentials and their relationship to the female menstrual cycle, also reported some startling findings of his own regarding the effects of the moon on plant growth.

Dr. Burr had begun his experiments in a modest way, choosing for his first subject a young robust maple tree that happened to be located outside his house in New Haven, Connecticut. To prepare the tree, Dr. Burr carefully stripped the bark and placed one small plaster container next to the tree one foot above ground level and a second container four feet above ground. Inside the containers were specially prepared electrodes surrounded by salt jelly. The upper electrode was connected to the positive terminal of a voltmeter while the lower electrode was connected to the negative terminal and was grounded.

Dr. Burr made no actual measurements of the tree's growth. However, it is known that trees give off minute electrical currents and that sharp increases in these currents are correlated with increases in physical growth. Consequently, any changes in the electrical potential of plants connected with the lunar cycle would constitute support for the moon's alleged influence on plant growth. After examining and analyzing detailed records of the systematic periodicity in the electrical activity of the tree over a three-month period, Dr. Burr found definite evidence linking that periodicity with the cycle of the moon. Interestingly, the greatest amount of electrical activity, and hence physical growth, was found to occur around the time of the full and new moon!

Further tests were then conducted. Not one to go too far afield when he didn't have to, Dr. Burr next wired up a rather ancient elm tree located outside his laboratory and an alligator pear tree located in the laboratory itself. Burr now had three "antennae to the universe" as he liked to call them, one located in the city, one in the country, and a third in the controlled environment of his laboratory. Once again, the trees indicated that their growth rates were directly connected with the cycle of the moon, thus corroborating Kolisko's earlier work.

More recently, Professor Frank A. Brown of Northwestern University in Illinois has also begun to study the relationship between the lunar cycle and plant growth, and he too has found several instances of a lunar-related effect on plants.

Dr. Brown began his experiments in this area by heading out to the grocery store and buying a number of Idaho potatoes. It was his intention to study the oxygen consumption of these tubers to see if their breathing rate was affected by the moon.

All living things, plants as well as animals, must breathe oxygen to stay alive, a process called respiration. During respiration, oxygen is taken into cells and is combined with sugar to produce energy. In the process, carbon dioxide is given off. Were it not for respiration, the cells of living organisms would not be able to produce the energy they need to function and death would occur. All living things breathe and continuously use up oxygen. This is why plants are usually removed from a patient's room in the hospital at night. If this were not done, the plants would remove some of the oxygen from the room and for some patients this could be dangerous.

During daytime, however, in addition to using up oxygen, many plants also manufacture oxygen during a process called photosynthesis. Through a complex chemical chain, which takes place in plants only in the presence of light, carbon dioxide is taken in and is combined with other molecules to make sugar. During this amazing process, oxygen is given off as a waste product. Thus plants are really self-sufficient. They are able to manufacture sugar, and they are able to use that sugar to do work. Animals, although much more complicated in many ways, are not so self-sufficient. They have to rely on plants for their source of sugar either directly or indirectly, by eating other animals that eat plants.

Fully aware of the oxygen requirements of plants regardless of whether it is day or night, Brown had the brilliant idea of measuring the daily respiration rate of the potatoes to see if this rate was affected by the cycle of the moon. The potato was a good specimen, since it grows below the ground and could be kept in a lightproof room. Accordingly, Brown hermetically sealed the sprouting potato tubers in a special apparatus in his laboratory and began collecting data. The experimental set-up was such that the sprouting potatoes were screened from environmental changes in light, temperature, air pressure, humidity, etc.—all sources of stimulation that could be expected to influence the respiratory rate of the plants.

The study itself extended over a ten-year period, and revealed that the respiration rate of the potatoes was greatest shortly before the time of the full moon and was lowest right after the new moon. In addition, there was also a daily lunar variation with a minimum respiratory rate near moonrise, and a maximum during moonset. "It seemed clear," concluded Dr. Brown, "that potatoes, therefore, even shielded for several months from variation in all ordinary environmental factors, persistently displayed apparently precise mean lunar-day and monthly periodisms."

In another study, Dr. Brown found a similar lunar-day and lunar monthly rhythm in the oxygen consumption of algae that clearly resembled that of the potatoes. Thus, despite differences in natural geographical locale, which placed the location of these experiments about a thousand miles away from the native home of the potatoes used, and despite the difference in species, one being terrestrial and the other marine, both the algae and the potatoes were characterized, by "an astonishingly similar lunar-day variation."

In still another experiment, Dr. Brown immersed baskets of ordinary garden beans in tap water for twelve to twenty-four hours. The baskets were then removed and pressed onto absorbent tissue and then weighed on a very delicate balance. After the weighing procedure, the baskets were resubmerged. After a further four hours, which was always timed to coincide with the noon hour, the baskets were removed, blotted, and weighed as before. The difference between the initial and the second weights was then calculated to determine how much water had been absorbed by the beans. Since the experiments were conducted in a laboratory in which the room temperature was always constant, there was no possibility that fluctuations in heat would affect the absorption of water by the beans. After a long series of studies in this specially designed laboratory, Dr. Brown found that the beans absorbed the greatest amount of water just before the time of the full moon and absorbed the least amount of water around the time of the new moon!

What is the explanation for this amazing action of the

moon on plant growth? Dr. Brown's studies show that the moon's influence transcends any obvious effect on the weather. It is as if there were some mysterious cosmic connection between the cycle of the moon and the growth of plants. We will come back to this mysterious cosmic connection in a moment. For now, however, let's examine how the moon affects plant growth outside the laboratory.

Earlier we mentioned that one of the ways the moon may affect plants is through its influence on rainfall. Although most meteorologists discount the ancient claim that the moon affects rainfall patterns, some of the more open-minded professionals who are less dogmatic in their thinking have been intrigued by the persistence of this bit of folk wisdom over the centuries.

One such group of professionals includes Drs. Donald A. Bradley and Max A. Woodbury of the University College of Engineering in New York and their colleague Dr. Glenn W. Brier of the Massachusetts Institute of Technology. Working as a team, these three scientists collected the records from 1,544 weather stations across the United States that had been gathering data on the weather since 1909. Next, they made a note of all those days on which it had rained throughout this long period and plotted these days against the position of the moon. To the surprise of the scientists, the graphs clearly demonstrated that it had rained more often on days around the time of the new and full moon than at any other time of the month.

Around the time that these American weathermen were studying this peculiar relationship between the moon's orbit and rainfall in the northern hemisphere, two Australian meteorologists, Drs. E. E. Adderley and E. G. Bowen of the Radiophysics Division in Sydney, were conducting similar inquiries in their part of the southern hemisphere. In agreement with their American counterparts, the Australians also found that it rained most often just around the time of the new and full moon.

When the two groups of scientists realized that they had been working on the same problem and had come up with the exact same findings, they agreed to publish their results simultaneously. In 1962, their two studies documenting the moon's influence on rainfall appeared in *Science*, one of the most prestigious journals in the scientific domain.

Here then was unquestionable proof that the movements of the moon influenced the weather. It made sense, therefore, to plant seeds around the time of the full moon, since it was more likely to rain at this time than at any other time of the month.

Farmers who have been planting by the moon by custom, have been convinced of the moon's influence on rainfall and have no need for scientific proof. The crops growing in their fields are proof enough. Nevertheless, it is gratifying to have an ancient custom hold up under the scrutiny of the objective eye of the dispassionate scientist. But those who plant by the moon have also been aware that it is not the moon's influence on the weather alone that is responsible for the superior growth of plants that are sown during the full moon. As Dr. Brown has learned from the many experiments he has conducted in his laboratory, the full moon also causes certain changes to take place in plants, enabling them to benefit maximally from this increase in rainfall associated with this particular phase of its cycle. The next question Dr. Brown and his colleagues must ask themselves is how the moon is able to orchestrate these rhythms in nature. The farmer who benefits from the moon's favorable influence may or may not care how the moon causes rain-bearing clouds to form or how it makes seeds absorb more water. But for the scientist, discovering the answer to questions such as these is an intriguing adventure. Proving that such a relationship exists is only the first step. Finding out how it works will lead him into new worlds of science never before imagined.

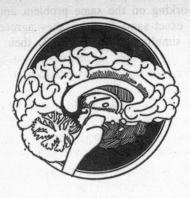

ONE of the oldest nervous disorders known to man is epilepsy; historically it is also the disease most closely associated with the moon. The oldest reference to this relationship between the two is more than three thousand years old and comes from an ancient Mesopotamian text which describes a man who is unconscious, his neck twisted to the left, his hands and feet tensed, his eyes widened and his mouth frothing, as one whose ailment is due to the "hand of Sin," the ancient moon god of the Near East.

Among the ancient Greeks, epilepsy was known as "the sacred disease" because of the belief that Selene, the goddess of the moon, had sent it to punish those who had sinned against her. "It is reckoned as a disgraceful form of disease," writes Aretaeus (first century B.C.), "for it is supposed that it is an infliction on persons who have sinned against the moon." So esteemed was the goddess of the moon to the Greeks that the philosopher Anaxagoras (500–428 B.C.) was sentenced to death in the city of Athens for dismissing the moon as nothing more than a lump of lifeless matter. In Rome, epilepsy was known as the "comital disease" because of the practice of suspending the Roman assembly (Comitia) if a member of the governmental body was observed to be suffering from an attack during a meeting. The reason for this adjournment was the feeling that a valid vote of all the members of the legislature would not be possible if one of the lawmakers was incapacitated by a seizure. In the Middle Ages, epilepsy became known as the "demon disease" because some individuals, among them Martin Luther, thought that it was a punishment placed upon certain men by the devil. Today, these socially ostracizing labels have all but disappeared, but the mystery, fear, and uncertainty that surrounded the disease in ancient days are still very much with us.

Although epilepsy, which means "to be seized" or "seizure," is spoken of as a single disease, there are actually a number of different kinds of epilepsies, each characterized by the severity of the observable seizure. The "grand mal" attack is the commonest form of the disease and accounts for about one-half of all "fits." It is also the kind of epileptic paroxysm familiar to most people because of the severity of the convulsions and the suddenness of the onset. Those experiencing "grand mal" attacks generally fall to the ground (hence the term "falling sickness"), their muscles firmly tightened. At the same time, their eyes may turn to one side and saliva may flow copiously from their mouths. Very shortly thereafter, their muscles begin to jerk violently. A few minutes later, the convulsions cease and the sufferer begins to recover.

The other main types of convulsive seizures are the "petit mal," which is characterized by a brief and hardly noticeable attack, and occurs mainly in children; the Jacksonian attack, which involves a brief loss of consciousness; and the psychomotor fit, in which involuntary muscle movements are observed, such that the sufferer appears to be reaching for imaginary objects in front of him. The last type of epileptic attack is the migraine headache, a persistent painful aching in the head which, like the other forms of epilepsy, comes on periodically and suddenly.

Although the cause of epilepsy is still unknown, in ancient times it was widely attributed to the moon's influence, and as a result, many of the remedies proposed for the treatment of the disease, in some way or another, contained some reference to the lunar cycle. For example, many people believed that mistletoe was a suitable therapeutic to cure epilepsy provided that it was gathered without the aid of an iron instrument, and provided it (the mistletoe) did not touch the earth, and especially provided that the leaves were gathered at the time of the new moon. Another popular remedy was to take coral, peony, and the root of strychonos (strychnine), place them in a linen bag, and hang them around the neck as an amulet to ward off attacks. According to the physicians of old, however, this would work only if the three items were collected at the time of the waning moon. Aelian, a third-century zoologist, repeats this bit of folklore but cautions his readers that should the plants be gathered after they have fallen to the earth, instead of being protected, the person being treated will die from the erstwhile remedy. Apparently, even pulling the peonies out by hand was to be avoided. Instead, Aelian gives this bit of advice: A young dog is to be starved until it is quite hungry. He is then to be tied to the peony plant, and food is to be placed out of his reach before him. When the dog goes after the food, the plant will be pulled out of the ground and then it can be safely used.

In her *Causes and Cures*, Saint Hildegard of Bingen (1098–1179 A.D.) advises her readers of another cure. A gem is to be placed in a pail of water for three days during the time of the full moon. This water is then to be warmed and kept so that the epileptic's food can be soaked in it during the waning period of the moon. Apparently, the idea was that the disease would disappear with the moon. However, this was not an overnight cure, for the same procedure had to be followed diligently for ten consecutive months.

Although epilepsy was still called "sacred" for quite some time, some ancient physicians soon began to propose explanations for its etiology which rested less on the supernatural and more on "natural" causal relationships. As an example of this new rationalistic approach we have the opinion of the author of the treatise *The Sacred Disease*, a work attributed to Hippocrates, that the disease of epilepsy was caused by the brain becoming unnaturally moist and flooded with phlegm. Several centuries later, we find Galen, the famous physician of Roman times, endorsing a similar opinion that epilepsy resulted from a heavy and chilly moisture in the hollows of the brain. Antyllus, his contemporary, concurred. "The moon rather moistens [the body]," he contended. "And for this reason it makes the brain relatively liquid and the flesh putrid and renders the bodies of people who live in a clear cold air moist and dull, and for the same reason, stirs up heaviness in the head and epilepsies." Oribasius, physician to Julian, a Roman emperor of the fifth century A.D., likewise attributed the moon's effect on the disease to its alleged moistening influence: "This too, we must mention," he states, "that the sun by its very nature heats the body, but the moon moistens it. For this reason the moon makes the brain more moist, rots flesh, causes the bodies of birds to become moist and sluggish and brings on epilepsy and dizziness."

Although he had little to say on the problem of epilepsy itself, Ptolemy, the renowned Egyptian astronomer, held the same general opinion concerning the moon's influence on the body. "Most of the moon's power consists of humidifying," he notes, "clearly because it is close to the earth and because of the moist exhalations therefrom. Its action therefore is precisely this, to soften and cause putrefaction in bodies for the most part, but it shares moderately also in heating power because of the light which it receives from the sun." Thus, "in its waxing from new moon to first quarter the moon is more productive of moisture; in its passage from first quarter to full, of heat; from full to last quarter, of dryness and from last quarter to occultation [*i.e.*, new moon] of cold."

This same opinion was still current in the seventeenth century as indicated by the medical texts of that century. For example, in one such work, published in 1627 by A. Spiegelus, students were taught that epilepsy was likely to be brought on at the time of the new moon because at that time the brain became dry and therefore the humors were not able to mix with the humidity. As a consequence, the brain became stretched and torn, a condition resulting in the seizures of the epileptic. The great German astronomer Johannes Kepler (1571–1630) likewise wrote that long experience had taught that all humors waxed and waned with the movements of the moon.

The conviction that the moon exercised an influence on the occurrence of epileptic seizures continued on into the Middle Ages and was not contested until the beginning of the eighteenth century, although there were disagreements as to the explanations behind its effects and therefore the kind of treatment to be employed to achieve the best results. On one side, there were still those who clung to the demonic theory and as a result prescribed for or treated the disease with magic, such as the protective amulet. On the other side were the so-called rationalists who accepted the lunar influence on the disease but looked for the "natural" causes behind those apparent effects. As long as magic and religion were not part of the cure, this latter group of physicians considered their treatments to be objective and free from superstition. Thus, in the twelfth century we find medical practitioners such as Arnald of Villanova declaring that epilepsy was a disease that was unquestionably under the influence of the moon and therefore ought to be treated with animal organs, precious stones, and other common curatives of the day, not because of any magic inherent in these materials, but because they had a natural, but as yet unknown, reason for their efficacy. This was also the opinion of the twelfth-century Jewish physician-philosopher Maimonides (1135–1204 A.D.). Writing in his *Guide for the Perplexed*, Maimonides freely admitted the magic element in many of the cures of epilepsy, such as that involving the plucking of peonies during certain phases of the moon. However, he also pointed out that the important aspect of this formula was not the magical element, but the fact that it was reputed to work. "For whatever is proved by experience to be true, although no natural cause may be apparent," he argued, "its use is permitted, because it acts as a medicine."

Many of these "natural" treatments were probably recommended on the theory that materials which were also subject to the influence of the moon, or resembled the symptoms of the disease, might have some sympathetic curative effect. For example, in the seventeenth century we find one Pierre Borrel prescribing the beneficial effects of powdered soapwart seed, which was to be used for three months at the time of the new moon. The reason for its recommendation was that when rubbed in water, it gave off a soaplike foam resembling the froth of the epileptic, and because it mimicked the disease in this way, Borrel felt it would have curative powers. It was for much the same reason that silver also came to be used in treating epilepsy. Because it resembled the moon in its pale, silvery color, it was thought that this particular metal was especially under the domain of the moon and therefore could be used in curing a disease which was also under the control of the moon. Accordingly, many an epileptic who came to a physician for treatment was advised to swallow silver filings. During the seventeenth to nineteenth centuries, these filings were replaced by silver nitrate (lunar caustic), especially in England, where it was employed unsparingly by many of the prominent physicians of that era.

In contrast to the medical approach, the magical treatment of the disease still involved conjuring out the disease from the afflicted body. One such spell that was widely used was as follows: "Take the sick man by the hand, and whisper these words softly in his ears, I conjure thee by the sun and the moon, and by the gospel of this day delivered by God . . . that thee rise and fall no more." While this magic did no good, it also did no harm. The same, unfortunately, cannot be said for those receiving the accepted medical treatment of the day.

In the eighteenth century, Dr. Richard Mead stated that during the time that he had been British surgeon in one of the many wars between the English and the French, he had had to treat so many young naval officers for epilepsy that he too was fully convinced of the moon's influence on the disease. "The power of the moon was so greatly felt," he wrote, "that it was not difficult to predict the occurrence of the attacks at the approach of the new or full moon." Mead, however, was not satisfied merely to make note of such instances, he also tried to account for this phenomenon. Uppermost in his mind at the time that he wrote these words was Isaac Newton's *Principia*, which first appeared in 1687 and which for the first time gave a rational explanation of gravitational forces, and in so doing also provided an explanation for the moon's influence on the tides. The same principles that Newton had brought to bear in explaining these phenomena, Mead reasoned, were applicable to the moon's influence on epilepsy.

As the years passed and physicians acquired more experience in treating diseases, many more doctors became convinced that the moon affected the human mind in some mysterious way and that in people suffering from epilepsy, the moon seemed to bring on their fits. In 1835,

Dr. J. Hunter told his pupils during a lecture that the "moon has certainly considerable effects on the human body. We find it often became the immediate cause of decreased actions, especially those of the mind." Hunter advised his pupils to take special notice of the moon in treating patients because of its influence on their bodies and on their minds.

Several years later, one of the most eminent physicians of the nineteenth century, Dr. M. H. Romberg, published a widely read textbook called *Manual of the Nervous Disease of Man*. In the course of his discussion of epilepsy, Romberg wrote that "the planetary influence of the moon (especially of the new and full moon) upon the course of epilepsy was known to the ancients, and although here and there doubts have been raised against this view, the accurate observations of others have established its correctness."

Romberg's reputation in the medical world was such that other doctors now began to consider seriously the moon's role in bringing on epileptic fits. Soon thereafter these physicians began to report evidence of their own that the moon had an effect on the epileptic.

In 1898, for instance, the Danish scientist Arrhenius reported that he had studied 9,000 cases of epileptic seizures and had found that a significant proportion of these seizures coincided with certain phases of the moon. Several years later, a German physician, Dr. Hellpach, likewise reported evidence of the moon's effect on the epileptic.

In 1947, an American physician, Dr. D. W. F. Petersen, published the records of a number of epileptic patients who had had seizures in 1930. These records clearly pointed out that there was, in Petersen's words, a "curious lunar rhythm" in the disease. This "curious lunar rhythm" was also corroborated by a Dr. M. Berg at the Kankakee State Hospital in Wisconsin, since a reexamination of his records also clearly showed that epileptic attacks occurred with greatest frequency around the time of the full moon.

Although most people who suffer from migraine headaches are not aware of it, the migraine attack is usually a form of mild epileptic attack. It differs from most epileptic attacks in that the sufferer does not have a fit, but nevertheless, the migraine is still considered to be a form of epileptic disorder. And like the major epileptic convulsion, it seems that the migraine headache, which causes excruciating pain, is also influenced by the moon.

One of the best-documented examples of migraine headaches being brought on by the moon can be found in the autobiography of the Swedish chemist J. J. Berzelius. Berzelius was one of the pioneers of modern science and was not one to jump at false conclusions. If he felt that there was some connection between two events, it was only after he had studied the relationship between those events for a long time. It is because of his meticulousness that his observations are worth noting.

Berzelius himself was plagued by periodic attacks of migraines, and in his autobiography he attributes his sufferings to the influence of the moon. "Since my twenty-third year," he wrote, "I had been tormented by a periodic headache, commonly called migraine. At first this occurred at long intervals but soon showed itself two times per month, falling with the greatest regularity on the day when the new moon or the full moon occurred."

Although it is not yet known for certain how the moon brings on these attacks, there is a certain amount of evidence from other areas of science that suggests that the changes in electrical potential associated with the full and new moon may precipitate these headaches. We have already referred to these changes in the electrical potential in the bodies of plants, animals, and humans in connection with plant growth and menstruation, and it is possible that this same effect may also hold in the present situation.

It has been found, for instance, that during sleep,

especially in the first few hours of sleep, the probability of occurrence of brain electrical activity characteristic of the epileptic seizure increases by about 100 percent. If at such times the epileptic is suddenly startled, as by a sharp noise, a seizure frequently occurs. This is thought to be due to the additional increase in electrical brain activity, which together with the hyperactivity already present in the brain, tends to raise the total brain activity above the threshold necessary for a seizure to take place. This seizure is thus produced as a result of additional stimulation from sound.

Seizures can also be brought on in the epileptic by having him look at light flashes. In ancient times, slave buyers made practical use of this observation and screened their prospective purchases for epilepsy by making them look at a rotating potter's wheel and its flashing reflection. Those slaves that suffered from epilepsy would often suffer an attack while they were staring at the light flashes, and when this happened the price paid for them would plunge.

It is for the same reason that some epileptics experience seizures while walking along a road which has closely spaced trees. On such streets the sun sometimes achieves a kind of flashing effect as the individual moves from one tree to the next, and this flashing effect brings on the seizure. Small children have likewise been observed to bring seizures on themselves by placing their hands in front of their eyes with their fingers spread apart, then moving them as they look at the sun.

Since it is known that immediately preceding the symptoms associated with epilepsy there is a large change in the electrical activity of the brain, and since such alterations in brain activity may be produced by light flashes, it is possible that the overstimulation caused by these flashes so excites the brain that the threshold for seizure activity is exceeded.

For the same reason, it may be that the full moon, by

increasing the overall electrical activity of the brain, may also bring on a seizure in the epileptic. This increased electrical activity connected with the appearance of the full moon may thus be the basis for the periodicity in seizures experienced by those unfortunate people who suffer from this "sacred" disease.

"NOT guilty by reason of insanity" is a verdict that judges or juries sometimes render in cases where a defendant is presumed not to have been in control of his senses when he committed an illegal and often terrible act.

The origins of this plea in medical jurisprudence go back to the eighteenth century, when the famous English jurist Sir William Blackstone defined "a lunatic, or *non compos mentis*," as "one who hath had understanding but by disease, grief, or other accident hath lost the use of this reason. A lunatic is indeed properly one that hath lucid intervals; sometimes enjoying his senses and sometimes not and that frequently depending on the changes of the moon." In other words, in the eyes of the law, lunatics were those who had lost their sense of right and wrong as a result of some influence exerted on their minds by the moon.

Another famous English jurist, Sir Matthew Hale, elaborated on this problem for the benefit of the courts in his discussion of the legal issues involved in an insanity or lunacy plea. Interpolated dementia, a term he used to express the idea that some people experience mental breakdowns periodically, "is that which is usually called lunacy," he said. He then went on to explain that "the moon hath a great influence in all diseases of the brain, especially in this kind of dementia; such persons commonly in the full and change of the moon, especially about the equinoxes and summer solstice, are usually at the height of their distemper."

Thus, according to these eminent legal authorities, lunatics were individuals who had their lucid moments during which they were fully aware of and therefore responsible for their actions. However, as a result of periodic lunar influences, they had a tendency to lose that clear-mindedness and self-control and under these conditions, they were no longer deemed to be responsible for their behavior. In contrast to the lunatic, the truly insane individual was always out of self-control, and therefore at no time responsible for his actions.

Since human lives not infrequently depended on a decision of whether or not there was a "lucid interval," the courts had to decide what constituted such an interval and what did not.

Pleading before the Parliament of Paris, the distinguished French jurist M. D'Aguessea argued that "to constitute a lucid interval there must not be a superficial tranquility, a real repose; there must be, not a mere ray of reason, which only makes its absence more apparent when it is gone, not a flash of lightning, which pierces through the darkness only to render it more gloomy and dismal, not a glimmering which unites the night to the day; but a perfect light, a lively and continued lustre, a full and entire day, interposed between the two separate nights, of the fury which precedes and follows it; and, to use another image, it is not a deceitful and faithless stillness, which follows or forbodes a storm, but a sure, steadfast tranquility for a time, a real calm, a perfect serenity, in fine, without looking for so many metaphors to represent our idea, it must not be a mere diminution, a remission of the complaint, but a kind of temporary cure, an intermission so clearly marked, as in every respect to resemble the restoration of health."

Although he did not explicitly mention it, one of the facts that also entered into a decision about whether or not a defendant experienced "lucid intervals" was whether or not his mental state changed at all during the full moon. If the moon were full at the time he committed his crime, such a fact could be entered as evidence that he was not in control of his senses since attacks of lunacy were, as Blackstone and Hale had said, noticeably brought on during certain periods of the moon.

Although the courts now speak of insanity instead of lunacy, the moon is still cited in some trials as one of the factors influencing the behavior of a defendant. These cases will be examined in the next chapter.

While the courts have only recently put their stamp of recognition on the moon's influence on the mind, the idea has been recognized throughout the long history of human existence.

As early as the fifth century B.C., for instance, we find the author of the ancient Greek medical treatise *The Sacred Disease* writing that "as often as one is seized with terror and fright and madness during the night and leaps up from his couch and rushes out of doors he is said to be suffering from the visitations of the moon." Centuries later poets such as John Milton wrote of "demoniac frenzy, moping melancholy, and moonstruck madness," and writers such as Shakespeare explained murder as "the very error of the moon, she comes more near earth than she was wont, and makes men mad."

In the French province of Brittany, peasants used to believe that if their women exposed the lower parts of their bodies to the light of the moon, especially during its first or last quarters, they would become "mooned," and would give birth to a child destined to become a lunatic. A similar belief kept German women from staying out at night on moonlit nights.

The universality of the belief in the moon's influence on the mind is also apparent from even a cursory survey of the languages of various nations of the world. For example, the Latin word *lunaticus*, the French terms *avoir des lunes* and *lunatique*, the German word *mondsuchtig*, the Latin word *luniatico*, and our own English word "lunatic" all refer to one who is insane by virtue of the influence of the moon.

During the early centuries of Christianity, the Church Fathers were somewhat upset by all the attention being given to the moon in the daily lives of the people in the Roman Empire. The Church saw the importance which the common people placed in the moon as a threat to its teachings that there was only one god. The people seemed to be attributing divine powers to the moon, and this had to be stopped. But although they did not themselves regard the moon as divine, the Church Fathers did recognize the influence of the moon on the human mind. St. Jerome (fifth century A.D.) tried to alter the common opinion that the moon itself caused men's minds to go astray by arguing that "lunatics are not really smitten by the moon, but are believed to be so, through the subtlety of demons who by observing the seasons of the moon strive to bring an evil report against the creature, that it might redown to the blasphemy of the Creator." In other words, Jerome wanted the people to believe that the moon was controlled by demons who were in league with the devil, and it was they who made the moon rob men of their minds. The moon was only the instrument of their evil ways.

Jerome's explanation seems to have fallen on deaf ears, for in the twelfth century, a certain Giraldus of Wales felt the need to repeat the Church's official explanation that the moon itself was powerless and that any effect it had on the human mind was caused by the devil, who only used the moon to achieve his own ends.

Several centuries later, the author of the *Malleus Malleficarum*, a book dealing with the evils of witchcraft and tests that could be used to identify witches, felt that the common people were placing more faith in the heathen idea that the moon brought on lunacy directly instead of by the power of the devil, and that the Church had to take a more definite stand. Those who persisted in believing such ideas were warned that their souls were in danger of going to perdition. "There are two reasons why devils molest men at certain phases of the moon," the writer explained. "First, that they may bring disrepute on a creature of God, namely the moon . . . Secondly, because they cannot, as has been said above, operate through the medium of the natural powers . . . Certain men who are called lunatics are molested by devils who would not so behave, but would rather molest them at all times, unless they themselves were deeply affected by certain phases of the moon. It is proven again from the fact that Necromancers observed certain constellations for the invoking of devils, which they would not do unless they knew that those devils were subject to the stars." By such circuitous reasoning, the Church felt that the influence of the moon on mankind was being minimized.

The Church, however, never had much success in convincing people that the devil was responsible for the actions of the moon. But while most people were more interested in what the moon did to men's minds, a few people began to ask how the moon exercised control. One of those who sought the answer to the secret behind the cosmic connection between the moon and the human brain was a Swiss physician of the sixteenth century, Theophrastus von Hohenheim, better known as Paracelsus.

Paracelsus was a veritable scientific jack-of-all-trades. His curious mind roamed the many avenues of the world of science, always searching for the reasons why things did what they did. As a physician, he was of course, particularly interested in the workings of the human body and in ways to cure it of disease.

When Paracelsus started studying mental illness, he was faced with not one, but five different types of people who were said to be insane from the medical point of view. These were the *Insani*, the *Vesani*, the *Melancholici*, the *Obsessi*, and the *Lunatici*.

The *Insani* were the congenitally afflicted. They had been born mad and had inherited the disease from their parents. The *Vesani* were those who had brought madness upon themselves as a result of bad habits such as eating excessively, eating contaminated food, and excessive drinking of alcohol. The *Melancholici* were those who had something in their character or personality that predisposed them toward madness. The *Obsessi* were those "obsessed by the devil." Finally, the *Lunatici* "are those who get the disease from the moon and react according to it."

According to Paracelsus, the mental aberrations of the *Lunatici* came about as a result of the ability of the moon to "tear reason out of man's head by depriving him of humors and cerebral virtues." This tearing-out process he likened to the ability of a magnet to attract iron. This "power of attraction," he said, "is at its height during the full moon, and therefore it attracts more strongly and the lunatics suffer most then." Moreover, because of the waxing and waning nature of the moon's appearance, Paracelsus pointed out that the strength of its powers of attraction would also wax and wane and that this would have important consequences in symptomatology. When the moon was in its new phase humor was drawn out from the brain, but this was not the same humor as that drawn out by the full moon. The full moon, which appears "rough and hard," attracts and draws out the "rough and hard humor"; the new moon, by comparison, "attracts only the fine humor." "While the moon exerts its attraction, as long as there is humor in the head it will draw it out," Paracelsus asserted. "This is the main reason for its drawing out and attracting most at the end of its period, and this explains why the end is most troublesome for those who begin the sick days of their nature during the moon."

In accounting for the moon's effect on lunacy, some medieval physicians had begun to speculate that the moon somehow increased the moisture of the brain in the same way that it caused the dew, and that this increased wetness was at the root cause of insanity. Paracelsus was one of the leading proponents of this view. "The *spiritus vitae cerebri*" of an insane person may be attracted towards the moon in the same manner as the needle of a compass is attracted towards the pole," he contended, "and such a person will, therefore, especially at the time of the new moon, when the attraction is strongest, grow worse and begin to rave; and likewise the *spiritus sensitivus* of a man is weak and offers no resistance and may be attracted towards the moon and be poisoned by its evil influence. The moon's influence is cold, and insane people have been called 'lunatics' because they were often imperiously affected by the moon whose influence acts upon the brain and stimulates the sexual passions and causes injurious dreams and hallucinations."

Having discussed the causes for lunacy, Paracelsus now proposed the cure. Since the moon acts like a magnet, and since the power of the magnet over iron and steel can be taken away from it by covering those objects it attracts with substances such as oil of mercury, it should also be possible to treat those suffering from lunacy with medicines which would prevent the moon from attracting their brain humors.

Paracelsus was one of the first scientists to consider seriously how the moon affects the human mind. Although his explanations were highly fanciful, he did interest other scientists in the mysterious link between the moon and human behavior, and it was not long before these other scientists began to examine the phenomenon and to discuss it with their colleagues.

One of these early scientists who became interested in this phenomenon was the famous physicist and chemist Robert Boyle (1627–1691), the founder of the Royal Society of England. Boyle was what might presently be called a "hard-nosed" scientist. It was not his way to go off half-cocked at any idea that crossed his mind. He usually thought deeply about anything he worked on, and so when he began to take an interest in the moon's influence on the human mind, he did so with the feeling that such an influence did in fact exist.

The problem for Boyle, however, was how to go about studying this phenomenon. Fortunately, or unfortunately, depending on one's own personal viewpoint, Boyle had a friend, "an intelligent person . . . [who suffered] a very dangerous fall, [and] so broke his head, that divers large pieces of his skull were taken out." This friend became Boyle's guinea pig, so to speak, since Boyle carefully recorded the observations of the surgeons who worked on his friend and also recorded his friend's own feelings.

Boyle noted that his friend complained about extraordinary "prickings and shootings in the wounded parts of his head" around the time of the full moon. At such times he would be in so much pain that he could not sleep. But once the full moon had passed, the pain disappeared and he had no trouble falling asleep. Furthermore, the surgeons themselves were astonished to see what they claimed was an actual expansion of brain tissue during the full moon!

This is not the only instance of a recorded change in brain tissue during the full moon. In 1627, a Dr. Adrian Spiegelus published a work on anatomy in which he stated that the brain swelled at the full moon. Whether he himself had witnessed any such swelling is not known, but in light of this change in the brain, he urged his colleagues that they consider the phase of the moon before contemplating brain surgery for any of their patients. Since the brain seemed to increase in size during the full moon, he advised his colleagues to perform their operations at this time since the brain would be closer to the skull and could be operated on more easily.

For its part, the medical profession remained fully convinced that the moon was in some way connected with mental illness, but no one seems to have looked for the reasons behind this influence to any great extent. Yet the medical textbooks were filled with advice to would-be doctors to pay attention to the moon in their treatment of the mentally ill.

"Mad people are certainly more affected at particular periods of the moon than at other times," wrote the English physician, Dr. John Hunter in 1835. "The full of the moon has the greatest effect," he contended, for "it not only affects those who have a natural predisposition but also some who have injuries done to the brain by external violence."

In France, Dr. M. Daquin wrote a famous treatise on the basis of his work at the mental hospital at Chambery in which he stated categorically that "insanity is a disease of the mind upon which the moon exercises an unquestionable influence. Those who are still susceptible of being cured, as well as those who have been cured," he wrote, "are precisely those upon whom the two most powerful lunar phases have had the greatest influence during the whole of their illness.

"Those who are acutely maniacal," he continued, "are much more susceptible to the influence of the lunar phases than others. I have also observed a difference between the influence exerted by this planet on madness characterized by excessive joy, and that by sorrow and melancholy."

In 1812, the celebrated American physician Dr. Benjamin Rush published his own views on the relationship between the moon and mental illness in a treatise entitled *Medical Inquiries and Observations upon the Diseases of the Mind*, a book that was to influence the practice of psychiatry in the United States for the next fifty years. Dr. Rush's credentials were impeccable. In addition to a thorough medical training in both the United States and Europe, he had been a signator of the Declaration of Independence, physician-general to the Continental army, and director of the Philadelphia Mint. Later on in his career he accepted the position of Professor of Medicine at the University of Pennsylvania, one of the leading medical schools in the country at that time. It was thus with great interest and regard that his colleagues and students considered any and all of his opinions relating to medicine or other matters.

Regarding the problems and controversy surrounding the influence of the moon, Dr. Rush wrote, "There is, I believe, an equal portion of truth on the side of both these opinions. In order to reconcile them, it will be proper to remark first, that in certain diseases and in certain debilitated states of the system, the body acquires a kind of sixth sense, that is, a perception of heat and cold, of moisture and dryness, of the density and rarity of the air, and of light and darkness, of which it is insensible in a healthy state. The moon, when full, increases the rarity of the air and the quantity of light, each of which I believe acts upon such people in various diseases, and, among others, in madness. A predisposition to the action of such feeble causes is required in all cases. From the conversion of excitability into excitement in mania, and from its absence in manalgia, it is easy to conceive, in both those states of derangement, the system will be insensible to the influence of the moon."

Although convinced that the moon's effect on the human mind was real, physicians such as Dr. Rush felt that there was no mystery involved. Rush believed that it was nothing else but the light of the moon that agitated patients.

The French physician Dr. E. Esquirol agreed with his American colleague regarding the moon's influence on the insane. "It is true that the insane are more agitated at the full moon," Esquirol told his students, "but it is the light of the moon that excites them, not any devils or supernatural powers." In Germany, Dr. W. Griesinger, professor of medicine at the University of Berlin, came to the same conclusion in a widely circulated medical textbook of the last century, *Mental Pathology and Therapeutics*. "With regard to the influence of the moon . . . even in healthy persons the light of the moon can peculiarly affect the course of thoughts, giving rise for example, to ardent and religious ideas readily disposing to sentimental poetry. In the insane, who are more powerfully and differently affected than the healthy by various sensible impressions, this may, with the absence of sleep, the view of the full and brilliant moon, the uncertain light, the fleeting shadows of the clouds combined with the stillness of the night, or the confused murmurs which then float through the asylum, indeed, create still greater impressions, more violent emotions, various hallucinations, etc."

The idea that the light of the moon was responsible for agitating the mentally ill became the accepted medical explanation for the observation that the full moon caused some people to lose control of their senses. Once this idea was accepted, the medical profession felt that the whole matter should be laid to rest and that it was imagination and superstition that caused certain people to act peculiarly, not any mysterious force emanating from the moon.

It is very often the case with superstition, however, that

what is regarded as nonsense by even the most respected of scientists turns out to be factual and true. George Sarton, the dean of historians of science, gives an interesting example of one such error in the case of Galileo, the inventor of the telescope, who "anxious to avoid astrological superstitions, flatly rejected the possibility of a lunar influence upon the tides . . . Here was one of the best intellects of all ages," Sarton notes, "but for once his passion for rationalism had led him astray, even as innumerable men had been deceived by their irrational love of mystery. Rationalism had led him to prejudice which is hardly better than superstition."

Although many physicians would probably do their utmost to avoid any association with "superstition" in their medical practices, it is interesting that scientific curiosity still drives some physicians to examine what their colleagues dismiss outright as astrological nonsense. Neither a mystic, an astrologer, nor a believer in the supernatural, Dr. E. Beamer-Maxwell of the Eastern State Hospital at Williamsburg, Virginia, along with her colleague, Mrs. M. F. M. Hendrick, a retired mathematical astronomer who had previously been connected with the U.S. Naval Observatory, decided to see whether or not there were more hospital admissions to the ward for the mentally disturbed at certain times during the cycle of the moon. These investigators must have known that what they were doing would probably earn them a lot of ridicule on the part of the hospital staff, but they decided that they were courageous enough to absorb it.

After poring over hundreds and hundreds of records covering a ten-year period, and plotting the number of admissions to the hospital versus the cycle of the moon, they were not a little surprised to discover that there were in fact significantly more patients admitted to the hospital around the times of the new and full moon than at any other period in the lunar cycle.

When the two scientists presented the results of their

findings to a meeting of the Virginia Medical Society in 1951, they aroused a great deal of interest on the part of the physicians in the audience. Many could not believe that the "superstition" was actually true, despite the evidence. Passing the report off as a fluke, they went on ignoring the medical records their colleagues had just presented.

Perhaps as disturbing as the report that more people were admitted to the hospital during the full moon was the finding that there was also a significantly greater number of people coming into the hospital at the time of the new moon. This latter discovery meant that the physicians of the last century, such as Rush, Esquirol, and Griesinger had been wrong in attributing the moon's influence to its light. This might explain why there were more admissions during the full moon, but it could not explain why the admission rate also went up during the new moon, when there was a minimal amount of moonlight.

In 1968, Dr. R. D. Osborn reported the results of a comparable study of patient admissions at a hospital in Uphan Hill, Ohio, between December 1964 and December 1965. Again a significantly greater number of patients were admitted to the psychiatric ward during particular phases of the moon than at other times.

In Texas, Dr. A. D. Pokorny came up with a similar finding regarding the relationship between admissions to mental hospitals throughout the state and the cycle of the moon. There was no doubt, then, that the moon did affect certain people in such a way that they seemed to behave peculiarly, irrationally, and even insanely.

In light of this evidence concerning patient admissions and the lunar cycle, hospitals could now plan their work schedules so that more staff would be on hand during the busy periods of the month, when the moon was "full" or "new."

These reports also led other scientists to try to find

out what it was that the moon actually did to certain people that made them temporarily unbalanced.

One such series of studies is presently being conducted by Dr. L. J. Ravitz, a neurologist at Duke University in North Carolina. We have previously encountered Dr. Ravitz in connection with his studies of the female menstrual period and his discovery of the changes in electrical potential that were associated with the menstrual period in women. Before we examine Ravitz' work, however, we will have to digress momentarily and talk about another scientist whom we have previously met—Dr. Harold Burr of Yale University.

Dr. Burr, as we have mentioned, demonstrated that all living organisms radiate an electric field. Beginning with such organisms as the salamander, he showed that when such primitive creatures as these are placed in a dish of salt water, they produce an electrical current just as a dynamo produces electricity.

Basically, a dynamo is nothing but a coil of wire rotating in a magnetic field. Every time the coil makes and breaks the field it produces an electric current. In his laboratory, Dr. Burr substituted salt water for the wire, since like wire it is a good conductor of electricity. After making this substitution, he rotated the dish of salt water with the salamander in it. If the salamander was emitting an electrical field, Dr. Burr felt that like a dynamo, it would generate an electrical current.

When electrodes were placed into the water and the wires run through a galvanometer, sure enough, the indicator moved to the left and then to the right, showing that indeed the salamander was generating electricity. When Burr removed the salamander from the dish and rotated the dish alone, no electricity was produced. With this simple apparatus, Dr. Burr had been able to demonstrate that even organisms as primitive as the salamander were able to produce electrical currents.

Once he had proved his theory, Dr. Burr then set

about making modifications in his testing equipment that enabled him to extend his studies to all kinds of plants and animals, including people. As a result of these pioneering studies, scientists now recognize the fact that all living organisms give off electrical fields.

But not only do living things produce electricity, they are also influenced by electrical fields into which they may wander or be deliberately placed, as in a laboratory. Living things thus both contribute to the electrical energy in nature and are in turn affected by nature's electrical fields.

Following Dr. Burr's lead, other scientists began to explore how the changes in a person's electrical output reflected his health and mental well-being and also how placing someone in an electrical field and thus changing his body's electrical potential would affect his health and mind.

One more interesting facet of this peculiar phenomenon should be mentioned before we continue, and this is that the earth itself acts like a dynamo and produces a small electrical current which affects us all. The strength of this electrical field, it should be noted, varies according to the position of the moon!

With these interrelationships in mind, Dr. Leonard Ravitz has been studying the behavior of patients in mental hospitals to see if their electrical potential and their behavior both change in synchrony with the phases of the moon.

After examining and studying such relationships for years, Dr. Ravitz is fully convinced that the brain's electrical potential does change rhythmically in connection with the cycle of the moon. One psychotic patient, whose brain gave off its highest voltage at the new and full moon, Ravitz says, also "felt like preaching and was increasingly grandiose, tense and irritable," at the same time as the electrical changes occurred in his brain.

Dr. Ravitz has used the same method to test student volunteers over a three- to eight-month period and has found similar changes in their brain waves which were closely correlated with the phases of the moon. These volunteers, however, did not suffer psychotic episodes at these times, indicating that while brain potentials do change in conjunction with the moon, it is only in people who are mentally ill that these changes result in outbreaks of bizarre behavior.

"Whatever else," writes Dr. Ravitz, "a scientific explanation is at last furnished for certain aspects of age-old myths ascribing various changes in state function to the lunar cycle."

Thanks to Dr. Ravitz, Dr. Burr, and many other scientists whose names we have not mentioned, the ancient belief in the moon's influence on the insane has been proved. The power of the moon to agitate the minds of certain people cannot be denied. There are more admissions to the psychiatric wings when the moon is full, and the people already in the hospital for mental problems also begin to act peculiarly at these times. We have just seen that the reason for this increase in abnormal behavior has to do with the moon's ability to alter the earth's electrical energy and the sensitivity of certain people to these changes.

Sometimes the "lunatic" simply becomes disoriented, or begins to have grandiose thoughts about himself. He may begin to think he is Jesus or Napoleon or some other great historical personage. These thought disorders which come and go with the passage of the moon do not arouse too much attention outside of one's family or the mental hospital in which a patient has been placed. But there is another thought disorder which does arouse general public notice. When the "lunatic" begins to feel that everyone is out "to get him" or that he is unable to control his actions and has an irresistible impulse to

"get someone," then his actions become a matter of concern for everyone, for there is no telling who will wind
up as a victim of this madman.

SEVERAL years ago, Thomas P. Brophy, Chief of New York City's Bureau of Fire Investigation, claimed that his experience had taught him to expect more fires on nights when the moon was full than at any other time of the month. During such times, he and his men maintained their most watchful state of alert, waiting for the inevitable rash of fires they knew they would be called upon to fight.

In England, London's *Daily Mail* reported an interesting case that had come to trial in the city of Birmingham. A twenty-three-year-old aircraft operator who had been absent without leave the Royal Air Force and was subsequently caught stealing money and was sentenced to six months at hard labor by the judge. Apparently the only testimony that was offered on his behalf was his mother's sworn statement that "his father always went wrong when the moon was full, and it affects this boy the same way when it is on the wane."

Among the crimes most dreaded by mankind is murder. The taking of a human life is considered to be the most desperate and the least tolerable of crimes and has been treated accordingly in the courts. Since murder has also been regarded as a crime of passion in most instances, it is not uncommon for jurists to take into account the mental state of the accused. And in such circumstances, it is also not uncommon to find reference to the moon as a factor contributing to the occurrence of the crime. For instance, in a trial described by the New York *World-Telegram* several years ago, the courts allowed the defendant to plead guilty to a lesser charge in response to a plea from a lawyer that his client "suffers periodic 'mental explosions' especially when the moon is full."

In 1961, Inspector Wilfred Faust of the Philadelphia Police Department filed a report with the American Institute of Medical Climatology. According to Inspector Faust, "The seventy-odd policemen who deal with telephone complaints have always reported that activity, especially crimes against the person, seemed to increase as the night of the full moon drew near. People whose antisocial behavior had psychotic roots—such as firebugs, kleptomaniacs, destructive drivers, and homicidal alcoholics—seemed to go on a rampage as the moon rounded, calming down as the moon waned."

Since the question of the moon's influence on insanity has greatly interested scientists throughout the ages, it is not surprising that the relationship between the condition of the moon and crime, especially the crime of murder, has also been subjected to scientific scrutiny.

In 1972, two scientists, Drs. A. L. Lieber and C. R. Sherin, added documentary evidence that more murders are committed during the time of the full moon than at any other time of the month. Reporting their findings in the *American Journal of Psychiatry*, Lieber and Sherin state that out of a total of 1,949 murders in Dade County, Florida, which occurred over a fifteen-year period between 1956 and 1970, significantly more crimes of this type took place at the time of the full moon than at any other time of the month. Dr. Lieber calculated that the probability of this coincidence occurring by chance was less than three in a hundred! Drs. Lieber and Sherin have also examined the police records from Cuyahoga County, Ohio, and have observed a similar lunar-related pattern in the murder rate for this northern state as well, making it appear less and less likely that this correlation between the cycle of the moon and the taking of lives is merely a superstition or a vague impression formed by law-enforcement officers.

Since most murders are not carefully planned hired killings but are instead crimes of passion involving a momentary loss of control, some authorities consider them to be akin to temporary losses of sanity. The person who kills his wife, husband, or friend or the person who buys a gun and climbs to the top of a tall building and fires at anyone in sight very often does so because of an uncontrollable impulse. He or she has an uncontrollable urge to kill. There are actually many forms of antisocial behavior that occur as a result of poor impulse control. Some of these we have already mentioned, such as pyromania (the urge to set things on fire), dipsomania (the urge to drink excessive amounts of alcohol), and murder. Suicide, which we shall talk about shortly, is another act of mayhem associated with poor impulse control. In the case of suicide, however, the victim is oneself.

Many other forms of poor impulse control that do not lead to criminal or antisocial behavior. In fact, the advertising industry spends a great deal of time and money trying to discover what makes customers buy things on impulse. Supermarkets spend thousands of dollars each year hiring such agencies to tell them how to get more money out of the potential "impulse buyer."

People are subject to all sorts of impulses. Whether these impulses cause us to buy something we don't really want or need, or whether they cause us to pick up a

weapon and strike at someone for some insult imagined
or real, we are all creatures of impulse. Most of us,
however, are able to control our antisocial impulses
because of our training. We have learned to inhibit most
of our impulses. Sometimes, for instance, when we get
drunk, we suffer a loss of inhibition. Then we say or do
things that we would not ordinarily say or do.

The impulse to say or do such things, scientists tell
us, results from a loss of control by the higher regions
of the brain. These regions contain "inhibitory centers"
which through the long process of growing up develop
a special disciplinary function over our behavior. Psycho-
analysts refer to such functions as the "superego."

Psychoanalysis is a branch of psychiatry started by
Sigmund Freud. It was Freud's belief that human behavior is governed by three basic mental structures. One
of these structures is the "id," which is the animallike,
instinctual reservoir of antisocial activity. The id is that
part of humanity that wants to fight, and to destroy if
necessary, in order to satisfy its demands. The id is the
impulsive side of man. It wants immediate gratification.

The second structure is the "ego." It is responsible
for holding the impulsive id in check. The ego tries to
restrain the id whenever it wants to do something that
is contrary to the customs of society. The ego is the
restraining force. The third force is the "superego." It
represents the teachings of parents and culture. It is the
conscience. It watches over both the id and the ego. It
makes sure the ego does not weaken and let the id go
berserk.

In psychoanalytical terms, murder occurs when the
impulses of the id cannot be restrained. The ego and
especially the superego lose control. One way such losses
of control occur is through drunkenness. Another, it
seems, is when certain cosmic forces act on the brain
to weaken the normal inhibition it exerts over the id.

The moon, as we have seen, does peculiar things to

people. It causes them to act in peculiar ways. Earlier we saw that it causes a change in the electrical activity of the body. Since nerves are in many ways similar to conductors of electricity, it is quite possible that the moon drives some people mad or causes them to become so infuriated that they become dangerous to themselves and other people, because of changes in the electrical functioning of the inhibitory centers of the brain. For some people whose superegos are already weak, a slight push over the top would be all that was needed to make them lose control of their destructive tendencies.

FOR every 100,000 people living in the United States, eleven will take their own lives each year. This means that in a country such as ours which has a population of 200,000,000, there will be 22,000 deaths by suicide each year. These figures make suicide the twelfth leading cause of death in the United States and put it far ahead of the homicide rate. Even more shocking, perhaps is the widely acknowledged fact that these figures are too low. The actual number of deaths by suicide is more like 27,000 to 30,000 per year, whereas the number of attempted suicides is estimated to be eight times greater than the number of deaths. In other words, about one out of every 800 persons attempts to kill himself in the United States every year!

Throughout history, mankind has been puzzled and dismayed at the occurrence of self-inflicted death. A thousand years ago, the Roman statesman Pliny uttered a lament over the suicide of his friend Corellius Rufus which is as relevant to our time as to his. "Corellius Rufus," Pliny said, "has died, and died by his own wish, which makes me even sadder; for death is most tragic when it is not due to fate or natural causes. When we see men die of disease, at least we can find consolation in the knowledge that it is inevitable, but, when their end is self-sought, our grief is unconsolable because we feel that their lives could have been long."

Although many reasons have been cited in explaining why this desperate behavior occurs, at least one survey has concluded that 94 percent of all suicides, successful or aborted, are committed by individuals suffering from some sort of mental problem, usually depression.

The scientists who study suicides have distinguished between the motives and the actual causes of suicide. Motives can be situations such as unrequited love, marital discord, resentment, despair, loneliness, financial distress, etc. Causes, on the other hand, are internal factors of which the victim is often unaware. A change in one's body chemistry, for instance, can alter the hormonal balance, and this alteration may in turn affect one's feelings and disposition. The female menstrual cycle, which we shall talk about in a moment, is one such example of a change in the hormonal balance of the body that affects the mind of many women, causing them headaches, disturbances in thought processes, and often deep psychological depression. In fact, scientists have found that more women attempt suicide than men by a wide margin.

In light of the cyclic nature of many mental illnesses and the preponderance of attempted suicides by women versus men, a number of investigators have sought to determine whether the periodicity that is often seen in the suicide rate is correlated with the lunar cycle.

In "Moonlight and Nervous Disorders," an article that appeared in the *American Journal of Psychiatry*, Dr. J. F. Oliven briefly described one such study in which more than half of the reported suicides for a particular period were found to have occurred at the time of the full moon.

A study done in the city of Chicago by Dr. S. A. Levinson, the Chief Coroner, likewise showed that there was a marked tendency for certain individuals to kill themselves around the new or full moon rather than at some other time during the month.

In Buffalo, New York, Dr. D. Lester of the Suicide Prevention and Crisis Center studied the suicide figures for 1964 to 1968 in that city. In four of the five years examined, more suicides occurred around the full moon than at any other time of the month.

In 1972, two Australian scientists, Drs. L. J. Taylor and D. D. Diespecker, reported that there was a significant increase in the number of attempted suicides by women associated with particular phases of the moon. A Canadian study conducted by two psychologists, Drs. K. P. Ossenkopp and M. D. Ossenkopp, likewise reported that more women killed themselves by poisoning during certain phases of the moon. The coincidence could simply not be explained as a chance occurrence. The moon had to be having an effect on their desire to kill themselves.

12.   Lycanthropy
(The Werewolf Syndrome)

DURING the days of the Greeks and Romans and especially the Middle Ages, it was commonly believed that men could be transformed into animals, either as a result of their own magic, or by the power of evil spirits acting upon their unwilling bodies. As a result of this belief, the metamorphosis of humans into wolves became a frequent occurrence as men, thinking themselves wolves, began to act the part in a kind of self-fulfilling prophecy. In Transylvania, these creatures were called *volkodlaks*. *Loup-garus* was the French term, while in Scotland they were called *warwulfs*. Our own term "werewolf" comes from the German *werwolf*. "Were" itself means "man," and hence our word literally means "wolf-man" or "man-wolf."

The term "lycanthrope" is sometimes used as a synonym for "werewolf," but there is actually an important distinction between the two. Whereas "werewolf" generally refers to the fictional, the mythical, or the imaginary world of the occult, "lycanthropy" is a term used to designate an actual form of mental aberration in which the individual has delusions that he is a wolf. The word itself is derived from Lycaon, the king of Arcadia in Greece.

According to the story told by the poet Ovid in his *Metamorphoses*, one day Lycaon was host to the great god Jupiter and mischievously fed his guest a dish of human flesh to see if the god was as omniscient as he was supposed to be (and would therefore recognize the taste) or would be fooled into thinking it was the meat of an animal. Jupiter, however, was not fooled. Nor did he regard the test with amusement. Angered at the insult, he turned upon Lycaon and changed him into a wolf, and in Ovid's words:

> In vain he [Lycaon] attempted to speak; but from that moment / His jaws were covered with foam, and he thirsted only / For blood. As he ravaged among the flocks, panting for slaughter, / His garments were transformed into hair and his limbs became crooked. / Ancient looking as before, appearance rabid, / His eyes sparkled savagely, the picture of frenzy. (Met. 1. 237)

Side by side with this myth is another account in which Lycaon again is the main character. According to this legend, Arcadia was beset with attacks by ferocious wolves, and as the people were mainly pastoral, they suffered greatly. Thinking that their misfortunes were due to the disfavor of the gods, Lycaon, their king, decided that the best way to get back into the good graces of the gods was to offer them a sacrifice—and what more tender a morsel for a god than the flesh of a young child? As a result of this institution of human sacrifice and the name of the king, the story assumed the eventual format of a man changing into a wolf in order to feast on human flesh.

As early as the Roman era, however, lycanthropy was

recognized as a peculiar form of insanity. During certain times of the year, especially around February, certain madmen who suffered from this peculiar disease would take to the hills and live in the manner of wolves. From their lairs they would roam about at night attacking and tearing to pieces the bodies of all those who were imprudent enough to be out after dark. In other countries, werewolves were said to make their dens in cemeteries, where they slept in graves and glutted themselves on corpses when the living were not to be found.

An early case of lycanthropy is related by William Seabrook in his book *Witchcraft, Its Power in the World Today*. A Frenchman living on the Ivory Coast kept his wife in a cage because he believed her to be a werewolf. The cage itself was large and comfortable, and there was no indication of cruelty on the part of the husband. The wife herself refused to bring charges against her husband when given the change. Instead, she preferred to remain locked up, for whenever she was given her freedom, she always returned the next day with her jaws smeared with blood.

According to psychoanalytic opinion, lycanthropy derives from the same psychological imbalance as vampirism, namely the impulse for sexual pain and the fascination with the shedding of blood. Even before Freud, however, the celebrated nineteenth-century authority on the subject of lycanthropy Sabine Baring-Gould called attention to the sadistic side of mankind which "in common with other carnivora, is actuated by an impulse to kill, and by a love of destroying life.

"Often have I seen an eager crowd of children assembled around the slaughter houses of French towns, absorbed in the expiring agonies of the sheep and cattle, and hushed into silence as they watched the flow of blood."

According to Baring-Gould, the wish to inflict suffering on others exists in all of us; the only difference between one individual and the next is the extent or degree to which each is able to inhibit this impulse.

During the sixteenth century, all Europe was terror-struck by a plague of lycanthropy. Between 1520 and 1630 no less than 30,000 cases of the disease were recorded. In 1573, for example, the Parliament of Dole order a concerted effort "with kitchen-spits, halbreds, spears, arquebuses, and sticks to hunt, capture, bind, and kill the werewolf who infest the district."

For some unknown reason, the lycanthropy madness was centered mainly in France. The blood bath that occurred in France as a result of this plague eventually subsided, but instances of murder by men who believed themselves wolves still occurred until the last century on a rather wide scale.

When apprehended, these unfortunate creatures were either killed on the spot or else were led off in chains to insane asylums. The French psychiatrist Esquirol described those afflicted with this form of mental illness who came to his attention as follows: "These wretched beings fly from their fellow man, live in the woods, churchyards and ancient ruins, and wander, howling, about the country at night. They permit their beard and nails to grow, and thus become confirmed in their deplorable convictions, by seeing themselves covered with long hair, and armed with claws. Impelled by necessity or a cruel ferocity, they fall upon children, tear, slay and devour them."

The symptomatology associated with lycanthropy has more recently been described by Brian J. Frost as follows: "The lycanthrope is weak and debilitated with a gaunt, emaciated body. His legs are covered in ulcerated sores caused by frequent falls and through grovelling on all fours in wolflike posture. His face is deathly pale, the eyes dry and hollow yet blazing with a demoniac fury mirroring the bestial thoughts within his soul. Though his mouth is parched, he craves only for warm blood to quench his thirst."

In the Middle Ages, the cause of this affliction was believed to be some sort of disease which entered the body either as a result of being bitten or scratched by a werewolf or by eating the flesh of an animal previously killed by one of these creatures. If someone were even suspected of having been bitten or of having eaten such flesh, no chances were taken. The unfortunate soul was either killed on the spot by his frenzied neighbors or else he was chased into the hinterland.

Most of the time the werewolf was supposed to look and act as normal as anyone else. But during the cycle of the full moon the blood of the werewolf was believed to undergo a unique chemical transformation which caused his human body to metamorphosize into that of a wolf.

This change was thought to occur only at this period in the moon's cycle, and in many of the recorded instances of attacks by the insane, the full moon appears to have played a particularly important role in triggering the imaginations of those suffering from this mental derangement. This circumstance is echoed by the eminent anthropologist Sir James Frazer: "The bright moonlight which figures in some of these werewolf stories is perhaps not a mere embellishment of the tale but has its own significance for in some places it is believed that the transformation of werewolves into their bestial shape takes shape particularly at the full moon."

S. Baring-Gould also noted the importance of the moon, especially the full moon, in precipitating this bizarre phenomenon. In his *Book of Were-Wolves* he observed that "in the south of France (where lycanthropy became quite common beginning around the fifteenth century), it is still believed that fate had destined certain men to be lycanthropists—that they are transformed into wolves at full moon."

According to Montagu Summers, another eminent authority on the subject of lycanthropy, the people of Palermo, Italy, "say that as the moon waxes to her round [*i.e.*, the full moon] the werewolf begins to feel the craving; his eyes sink deep in his head and are glazed, he falls to the earth wallowing in the dust or mud, and he is seized with fearful writhings and pangs, after which his limbs quiver and contract horribly." Judging by this description, it would seem that the people of this area have witnessed epileptic seizures and in their ignorance they have attributed these attacks to the sufferings the werewolf is believed to undergo at the time of the full moon.

The role of the moon in lycanthropy is also illustrated by the following excerpt from a Russian incantation which was repeated by those who desired to transform themselves from their human forms into that of a wolf:

Moon, moon, gold-horned moon,
Check the flight of bullets, blunt the hunter's knives,
Break the shepard's cudgels,
Cast wild fear upon all cattle,
On men, on all creeping things,
That they may not catch the gray wolf,
That they may not rend his warm skin.

From the instant that the full moon first becomes visible in the sky until it finally disappears in the brightness of the sun, the werewolf is believed to become a restless hunter driven by an insatiable appetite for flesh. Come the daylight, however, this uncontrollable urge leaves him and his madness gives way to tranquillity. His behavior was thus believed to be utterly under the influence of the moon.

Still another component in werewolf folklore is the wolfbane plant, which is said to bloom only during the full moon in autumn, and which was reported to be the only cure for lycanthropy. According to some beliefs it was only when the wolfbane bloomed, in autumn during the full moon, that the transformation from man to wolf could occur, a belief that is echoed in an ancient gypsy rhyme:

> Even a man who is pure in heart
> And says his prayers by night
> Can become a wolf when the wolfbane blooms
> And the autumn moon is bright.

How this relationship between lycanthropy and the wolfbane plant arose is not known, although there is a plant called wolf's bane, or actually there are two plants with this name. The first, *Aconitum napellus*, as it is known in botanical Latin, grows in the mountainous regions of Europe and Asia. It is a very poisonous plant whose main ingredient, aconite, lowers blood pressure and slows the blood circulation. The second plant, *Arnica montana*, is also mainly found in Europe. The main use for arnica, the drug made from its flowering parts, is in the treatment of various palsies, but because it produces violent intestinal pains, its use is quite limited.

The subject of lycanthropy still captures the imagination of modern writers, although reported instances of the disease are rather rare today. Occasionally, it still turns up in some prestigious medical journals. For example, an article entitled "The Moon, Werewolves, and Medicine" by Dr. W. B. McDaniel appeared not very long ago in the *Transactions and Studies of the College of Physicians of Philadelphia*. The author states that he was particularly interested in the survival of the belief in lycanthropy since "Benighted members of backward communities, even within our own time, have believed that man may be made so wolverine under the influence of the moon as to act like wolves and even suddenly to grow nails of great length like to of the animal's claws.

"Persons who have the hereditary tendency to become wolverine should beware of the light of the moon at all times," according to the belief. "They must cover the face when they lie in bed," in order to avoid being so afflicted, but "if at some time before morning they might be struck by its direct rays," then the metamorphosis would be precipitated.

Although the origins of this folk belief that men can be transformed into wolves under the power of the moon is lost in the past, one may speculate that the barking of dogs and the howling of wolves at the moon may somehow have linked the canine to the moon, setting in motion a thought process that culminated in the werewolf legend. Once this legend gained popularity, the self-fulfilling prophecy began to operate—believing that they were destined to act like wolves, the mentally deranged began to act the part at the time of the full moon, a time at which their minds were most suspectible to the moon's mysterious forces.

AS early as 1838, reports began to appear in the scientific literature that the nocturnal ramblings of certain sleepwalkers (somnambulists) were induced by the light of the full moon, a phenomenon known as lunambulism. Richard von Krafft-Ebing, the celebrated psychiatrist of the nineteenth century, recognized the existence of the phenomenon, and contended that it was "a symptomatic manifestation of certain nervous diseases." Many of his colleagues, however, refused to recognize the phenomenon at all. Dr. H. Spitta, for example, denied its existence outright, contending instead that "the much discussed and romantically treated 'moon walking' is a legend which stands in contradiction to hitherto observed facts. That the fantasy of the German folk mind drew to itself the pale ghostly light of the moon and could reckon from it all sorts of wonderful things, proves nothing to us."

Nevertheless, despite Dr. Spitta's skepticism, lunambulism has been described by many eminent medical authorities, and in the words of Dr. J. F. Oliven, "although in recent years few such observations have been made, there seems little doubt that the phenomenon exists."

The most comprehensive examination of lunambulism is contained in a treatise by Dr. J. Sadger, a Viennese psychoanalyst, who gathered together case histories from his own medical practice and published them. Sadger's description of the phenomenon as observed in his patients is as follows: "Under the influence of this heavenly body [the moon] the moonstruck individual is actually enticed from his bed, often gazes fixedly at the moon, stands at the window or climbs out of it, 'with the surefootedness of the sleepwalker,' climbs up upon the roof and walks about there or, without stumbling, goes into the open."

After citing the example of one of his patients in detail, Dr. Sadger suggested that perhaps there was "more than a mere superstition behind the folk belief which conceives of a 'magnetic' influence by which the moon attracts the sleeper." Dr. Sadger suggests that the basis of this magnetlike attraction may be analogous to the way in which the moon influences the tides, or alternatively, there may be some direct effect of moonlight itself. "Such a relationship is indeed conceivable," he contends, "when we consider the motor-overexcitability of all sleep walkers and the effecting of ebb and flow through the influence of the moon. Furthermore, no one, in an epoch which brings fresh knowledge each year of known and unknown rays, can deny without question any influence to the rays of moonlight."

Although Dr. Sager's speculations seem a little farfetched, in point of fact, a number of controlled experiments conducted by Dr. L. W. Max have actually shown that light increases muscle movements in human subjects. This was demonstrated using rather sensitive electromyographic recordings of the flexores digitorum muscle of the arm which indicated a distinct muscle response to light. At the same time, in thirty out of thirty-three of the experiments conducted by Dr. Max, the subjects reported that they were dreaming when the stimulus was presented. This study is remarkable since it suggests that the light stimulus was perceived in some way by the sleepers and that this induced them to begin dreaming. The muscle responses may then have been associated with these dreams, but it is also possible that they were elicited independently of dream activity by the light stimulus. If so, it might then be conceivable that in cases of lunambulism, the light of the moon falling upon certain sensitive individuals may in some way elicit these muscular movements in other parts of the body in such a way that they begin walking in their sleep. There is, however, little evidence to support such speculation.

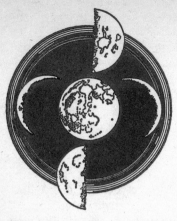

HOW is it possible for the moon to exert all these effects on plants, on animals, and on us humans? What conceivable sensory system do living organisms possess that is capable of receiving impulses from an object 239,000 miles away in space? What is the means of communication? Since the nerves of the body are the only channels we possess for gathering information from our environment, the moon must in some way affect our nervous systems. To understand how this is possible, we must familiarize ourselves with some of the basic facts about bioelectricity, the relationship between electricity and living organisms.

The discovery of bioelectricity has its beginning, like so many other monumental discoveries in science, in an accident. One day while he was working in his laboratory, the Italian scientist Luigi Galvani moved a frog's leg he was studying a little too near a wire and the leg twitched just as though it were still alive. Fascinated by this observation, Galvani repeated the experiment and once again the frog twitched. Flushed with enthusiasm, Galvani joyously announced to the scientific world that animal muscles generated electricity when they came in contact with metal. Another Italian scientist named Alessandro Volta, however, felt that there was a different explanation. The electricity didn't come from the frog's leg, he argued, but from the different kinds of metals the leg was in contact with. To prove his point, he built the first electric battery or "volt pile" consisting of layers of silver and zinc discs separated by cloths that had been soaked in brine.

We now know that Galvani and Volta were both correct. Animal muscle can produce electricity and also can be influenced by electricity. Science has come a long way since the time of Galvani and Volta. Studies of the electrical properties of living organisms are innumerable, and information on the subject is still filling scientific journals as we continue to learn more and more about bioelectricity. Today the experiments of these two pioneers in electricity are being repeated in high school and college science classes throughout the world. The once esoteric and unusual is now a commonplace laboratory exercise for students.

Once he had perfected his battery, Volta started a new series of experiments in which he touched the exposed wires from the battery to various parts of his body. When he touched his tongue, he experienced the sensation of taste; contact with his ears brought the sensation of sound. Volta had discovered the "specific doctrine of nerves" which states that no matter how a particular nerve is stimulated, once activated it carries an electrical impulse to the brain. The brain then interprets the message in a way that corresponds to the natural stimulus, e.g., light, sound, heat, etc., that would ordinarily be signaled by that nerve, and not according to the energy itself, in this case electricity.

Electricity can come from many sources. If you walk across a thick rug and then touch a metal doorknob, a TV dial, or the hand of a friend, you will suddenly become aware of static electricity when you get a brief and unpleasant shock. Lightning is another form of static electricity.

Electricity itself is nothing other than the movement of tiny negatively charged particles called electrons through a conducting material. This movement of electrons across cell membranes is the basis of all biological events in both the animal and the plant world. Activity in the human brain is characterized by a negative wave which passes briefly through the cell membranes, causing a flow of electrical current to pass through the cell. Some materials, like copper wire and nerve tissue, are good conductors, so electrons move through them very easily. Other substances, like rubber and wood, are poor conductors, so electrons have a hard time passing through them. Whatever the conducting material, however, there must be some force or pressure to drive the electrons in the first place, and this force is voltage. When there is an excess of electrons in one area and a deficit in another, a pressure is created such that the electrons try to move toward the part lacking in electrons. The strength of the pressure to do so is the voltage. When lightning occurs, there is an excessive negative or electron charge in the clouds relative to the earth, and when these electrons travel en masse to the earth, this is seen as lightning. In the nervous system, the sensory receptors produce their own voltage potential by reducing the positive charge which is normally present on the surface of resting nerve cells until a critically low level is reached. Once this depolarization occurs, a predetermined sequence of events takes place which basically involves the passage of a negative wave through the nerves. After the wave has passed, the positive charge is reestablished on the surface of the membrane. This rather simple but elegant biological mechanism of "depolarization" and "repolarization" of nerve-cell membranes is the basic process responsible for electrical activity in nerves and the consequent complexities of human, animal, and plant life.

Although the depolarization of nerves usually occurs as the result of stimulation of sensory receptors, *e.g.*, light striking the eye or sound being received by the ear, depolarization can also occur by direct electrical stimulation of nerve cells. As Volta showed many years ago, the sensations of light and sound can be experienced by simply touching an electrical wire to various parts of our heads. Mechanical stimulation can also cause us to see. To prove this is true, place your finger against your eye next to your nose and gently press. If you do this, you will "see" a black patch. Seeing "stars" as a result of a blow on the head is another instance of visual experience resulting from mechanical stimulation.

Very early in the history of modern studies in electricity, scientists discovered that magnetic stimulation could also cause electricity to flow and hence it was possible for magnetic stimulation to affect the nervous system. But before we examine this phenomenon, let us look for a moment into the nature of magnetism itself.

Suppose you were to place a sheet of paper over a bar magnet and then sprinkle iron filings over the paper. If you now gently tapped the paper, you would see the filings begin to arrange themselves in a pattern such that most of them would become concentrated near each of the ends of the magnet. The farther away from the "poles" of the magnet, the less dense would be the concentration of filings. This little experiment demonstrates that around every magnet there is an invisible "field" which exerts a force on every object that is brought near it. Although it was once believed that only those objects such as iron were affected by magnetic fields, we will see in the next chapter that even living matter is influenced by exposure to magnetism even though it is not visibly attracted to magnets.

In order for magnetic fields to be produced, one does not necessarily have to have a bar magnet. This was first demonstrated by the Danish physicist Dr. Hans Christian Oersted. Dr. Oersted was experimenting with electricity one day and by chance he happened to look at a compass that was near the table at which he was working. Noticing that the compass began to act very erratically whenever electric current was turned on, he began to investigate this peculiarity and finally came to the conclusion that all electric currents produce a magnetic field.

After Oersted discovered that electricity could produce magnetism, another brilliant scientist, Michael Faraday, asked himself whether the reverse was not also true: Could magnetism produce electricity? After some painstaking work, Faraday did indeed find that if a magnet could be made to move, it would produce an electric current. The faster the movement, or the stronger the magnet, or both, the larger the current that could be generated.

The existence of a magnetic field on earth is, of course, quite apparent from the behavior of the ordinary compass needle. Essentially, a compass is nothing more than a magnetized needle. When allowed to move freely, the needle invariably (and to the great relief of all those who have been lost at sea or in the woods) points in a northerly direction toward the earth's "magnetic pole." The magnetic pole itself is a point on the earth near the north pole, where the magnetic force of the earth is at its maximum. Violent disturbances in the earth's magnetism can often be observed by the oscillation of a compass needle. Very often these oscillations occur in conjunction with solar disturbances. The changes in the earth's field may be so great as such times as to induce electrical currents large enough to interfere with telegraphic communication. The movements of the moon also cause changes in the intensity of the earth's magnetic field. Although these are not as great as those produced by the sun during its violent outbursts, they occur more

regularly and more often, the high point coming around
the phase when the moon is full. These alterations in the
earth's magnetic field, as we have seen, can affect our
weather. Independent confirmation of the effect of the
earth's magnetic field on the weather has also recently
been reported in *Nature*, by Dr. J. W. King of the
Appleton Laboratory in England.

Why the earth acts like a magnet is still a mystery that
scientists have not yet solved, but act like a magnet it
does. Regardless of the cause of this terrestrial magnetism,
the fact is that the earth is one vast magnetic field with
two magnetic poles, one near the north pole, the other
near the south pole. It is also a fact that the sun and
the moon both contribute to the strength of the earth's
magnetic field, but in certain parts of the world, the
influence of these two celestial bodies is greater than in
other parts. For example, in Batavia, Germany, the
moon sometimes produces as much as a tenfold increase
in the terrestrial magnetism of that area, whereas at
Greenwich, England, the increase is only about twofold.
Daily records of the magnetic activity of the earth have
also shown that some areas of the globe remain relatively
"quiet" from day to day, whereas other areas frequently
experience magnetic "disturbances." Dr. King has also
pointed out that the intensity of the earth's magnetic field
has changed over the centuries, and with it, the climate
in various parts of the earth has also undergone dramatic
changes, some of which have played no small part in the
history of our civilization.

For example, the first discovery of America, as we now
know, was not made by Christopher Columbus in 1492
but rather by the seemingly fearless Vikings around 1000
A.D. Reaching out from the Scandinavian countries of
Europe, the Vikings set their sails to the winds and headed
out into the unknown empty ocean without map or compass to guide them. First they came upon Iceland and
then Greenland, easily conquering the native inhabitants

of these islands. Colonies were quickly established and more Norsemen left their native lands for the "new world." Some of the Vikings landed on North America and explored the new continent, but most of these pioneers were content to eke out a new life on Iceland and Greenland, leaving America for the next generation of Vikings. But as fate would have it, around 1400 A.D. the climate in the North Atlantic began to turn much colder. Eventually, the cold began to affect the health of the otherwise hearty Scandinavian populace and they contracted diseases such as rickets. Their physical stature began to diminish and they became weaker overall, until the native population, which had hitherto been a conquered people, now felt that the time for liberation had arrived. More accustomed and acclimated to the cyclic changes of the North Atlantic islands, the native inhabitants rose up against the Vikings and eventually killed them or drove them back to Europe.

Changes in weather have played an important part in other historical events as well. Puerto Rico, for instance, was once a British island and might still be so today had not the increasingly hot temperatures in the late sixteenth century raised the incidence of yellow fever, the disease which virtually wiped out the English garrison stationed on the island.

Although we do not have confirmation that changes in terrestrial magnetism were associated with these changes in climate, we do know that the earth's magnetic field in the northern hemisphere around 1600 A.D. was much different from what it is today and that during the period between 1500–1700 A.D. Europe went through a "Little Ice Age."

Large changes in the earth's magnetic field can thus affect man indirectly by changing his environment. But what about the direct effects of changes in terrestrial magnetism? Are living organisms sensitive to the changes in terrestrial magnetism which are caused by the moon?

As we have already said, an electric current is nothing more than the movement of electrons through a conductor. When an object comes in contact with a magnetic field, the electrons in the object get pushed sideways at right angles to the direction of motion of the magnet. This starts the electrons moving, and hence an electric current is produced. Thus, around every current-carrying wire, or around every rotating magnet, there is both an electrical and a magnetic field.

If the electrons in a wire are first accelerated in one direction and then accelerated in the opposite direction, these electrons will send out an energy field composed of pulses of electromagnetic waves. When other electrons are introduced into this electromagnetic field, such as the electrons in a TV antenna, they absorb some of this energy and are thus acted upon by the electromagnetic waves. At some frequencies, these waves get transformed into our TV picture. At other frequencies, they take the form of light, and at still other frequencies, they become X rays.

There are, in fact, about sixty different components of the electromagnetic spectrum, and visible light is but one segment of this continuum. The actual awareness of the existence of this spectrum of electromagnetic waves goes back to 1799 when the English astronomer Sir William Herschel conducted an experiment in which he passed a beam of white light through a prism, thereby causing it to separate into different colors. Herschel then placed a thermometer in the pathways of the different colors to see which would produce the highest temperature. After he determined that the red light at the one end of the color spectrum gave a higher reading than the violet light at the other end, he became curious to see if there would be any temperature readings from the area beside the red, even though there was no color to be seen. And sure enough, the thermometer not only registered an increase, it in fact gave a higher reading than

Herschel could obtain from the red light itself. These "infrared" rays could thus produce heat even though they could not be seen. Two years later, a German scientist, Johann Wilhelm Rittes, detected the existence of colorless waves on the side of the violet end of the spectrum. It is these ultraviolet rays that cause us to tan if we stay in the sun for a short time, or burn if we overdo it and stay too long in its direct light. In addition to burning our skins, electromagnetic rays in the ultraviolet range also cause ergosterol, a chemical in the skin, to produce vitamin D.

While electromagnetic radiation in the form of sunlight is essential to the growth of plants, different plants require different amounts of sunlight radiation to achieve their best development. Every amateur horticulturist knows which species of plant "likes" to stay by the window and which prefer the shade. In addition to the amount of sunlight, scientists have now shown that different frequencies or colors of light produce different results if plants and even animals are exposed to such specific kinds of electromagnetic radiation. In one interesting experiment, fifty guppies in an aquarium were kept under blue fluorescent light for nine hours a day. Another fifty were maintained under identical conditions except that they were kept under pink light. Dramatically, the guppies raised under blue light did not produce any offspring while those raised under the pink light produced the usual numbers. Chinchillas that are raised outdoors under natural light typically produce the same number of male as female offspring. Raising them under blue light results in their producing only females. Chickens and roosters, however, do worse with pink light than normal sunshine. When raised under daylight-white fluorescent light for twelve hours each day, all their eggs are fertile; raising them under pink fluorescent light results in all their eggs being infertile.

Even animals that are blind respond to different

colors. In one experiment, mice had their eyes surgically removed and after they recovered from the operation, they were placed in activity wheels and were kept there under different lighting conditions. Those raised under red light were the most active, those kept under yellow were second, and those maintained under blue were least active of all. Apparently, the different frequencies of electromagnetic radiation, which we call color, were able to affect their behavior even though these animals could not see! Evidently, the eyes are not the only part of the body that can sense electromagnetic light energy.

Electrical responses to light have in fact been detected in the skin of frogs, guinea pigs, rats, and several other species of animals. In May 1973, Drs. Marshall S. Harth and Marietta B. Heaton of the North Carolina Department of Mental Health reported the results of an experiment which showed that newborn pigeons responded to light even before their eyes opened. First the scientists showed that a five-second light flash would cause the still-blind squabs to raise their heads and shake them from side to side. To make sure that light was not entering the eyes of the squabs, they covered their heads with a black cape. Again the young pigeons responded to the light flash as before. It is evident, the researchers deduce from these experiments, that the skin is able to detect electromagnetic radiation in the narrow band of waves between violet and red light.

What these experiments mean, of course, is that the bodies of living organisms are responsive to energy from their environments in ways that are only now beginning to be appreciated. Up until only recently no one realized that skin contains electromagnetic-sensitive receptors which can markedly affect the behavior of animals and probably humans as well. The nature of these effects is only now beginning to be realized.

The amount of energy produced by an electromagnetic wave is inversely proportional to the length of the wave.

Long waves such as radio waves or visible light rays give off little energy and are stopped by our clothing or by protective shields. On the other hand, short waves such as the X ray, the gamma ray, or the cosmic ray, contain a great deal of energy and it is more difficult if not impossible to stop them from penetrating our bodies.

Scientists now assure us that electromagnetic influences have always been a permanent feature of our environment, and consequently it is not at all unreasonable to assume that these influences may have played some role in the evolution of life on this planet. If this is indeed the case, then as a corollary to this assumption, we should not be surprised to discover that these influences will be reflected in biological processes occurring in living organisms.

IN the previous chapter we noted that the earth is one vast magnetic field. The explanation for this is not known at the present time. Whatever it is that produces this characteristic geomagnetism, however, it is reasonable to assume that this is no recent peculiarity of our earth but rather that it has existed from the time that the earth first came into being. Given this assumption, it is also not unreasonable to assume that during the evolutionary process living organisms not only became accustomed to the influence of this magnetic field, but that in some species, certain biological activities may still retain a sensitivity to these minute changes in electromagnetism.

In trying to demonstrate this to be the case, however, the scientist is confronted with an apparently unsolvable methodological problem, namely, how to remove an animal from the earth's magnetic field, or else how to turn off that field so that any changes in its behavior can be examined under systematic alterations of the forces being studied.

One solution to this problem has recently presented

itself in the exciting accomplishments of the space program. It is now possible to launch rocket ships and satellites far off into space where they are free of the earth's magnetic influence. Possible though it is, this solution is not practical. It is simply far too costly for research studies of this kind.

The second alternative, that of turning off the earth's magnetic field, is not possible, of course. There is yet another alternative, however. This third possibility involves increasing the intensity of the magnetic field in a particular area by means of electromagnets. Basically, this involves placing a plant or animal, or some individual, for that matter, in an experimental chamber and observing its behavior under conditions in which the magnetic field in the chamber is activated and under conditions in which it is not. From experiments such as these, it may then be possible to reconsider the role of the moon on living organisms, since it too produces an alteration in the electromagnetic fields in which animals, including man, must conduct their everyday activities. Thus, by varying the magnetic field in the laboratory, it may be possible to duplicate one of the effects that the moon produces on our planet.

On the face of it, studies such as these appear odd because every schoolchild knows that magnets only attract metal objects. But as is often the case with such everyday experiences, these observations are of a kind that do not permit any real appreciation of potential changes in behavior that can be produced by extended exposure to a magnetic field. Indeed, contrary to expectations, detailed observations of the ways in which the presence of magnetic fields may affect the growth, development, and behavior of several organisms have proved beyond a doubt that prolonged exposure to a magnetic field can produce significant changes in species as primitive as bacteria or as complex and specialized as man himself.

From our discussion in the previous chapter, the way

in which magnetic disturbances affect living organisms should now be evident. Magnetic disturbances set electrical currents in motion, and electricity is the means by which living organisms, plants as well as animals, derive information from their surroundings.

While the bodies of animals and humans contain nerves which carry electrical impulses from hands, feet, skin, etc. to the brain and back again, what about plants? Plants do not contain nervous systems—or do they? Remember that electricity is nothing more than the movement of negative atomic particles called electrons.

All living cells, whether they be animal or plant, contain organic salts such as sodium chloride and water. Some of these sodium chloride molecules come apart in the water of the cell and split into positive sodium ions and negative chloride ions. Because of a peculiarity of living cells, the positive sodium ions are pushed out of the cell and more positive ions accumulate on the outside of the cell compared to its interior. This means that there is a separation of positive and negative ions across the cell membrane, and this causes a potential voltage difference, which as we have previously seen, is the basis for the flow of electricity. Thus, while plants do not have a nervous system, they are still capable of receiving and transmitting electrical impulses. This particular capability of impulse transmission was one of the chief characteristics that Charles Darwin felt plants shared with animals. "The most striking feature of similarity [between plants and animals]," he wrote in his book *The Power of Movement in Plants*, "is the concentration of sensitivity and their transmission of excitation from the part which received the stimulation to another part which comes into motion as a result of this transmission."

The sensitivity of plants to environmental stimuli was demonstrated as early as 1904 by the Indian scientist Sir Jagadis Chandra Bose. Using a special piece of equipment called a rescograph, which he himself invented, Bose was able to measure and record nervous activity in animals. By modifying his apparatus somewhat, Bose was also able to demonstrate that plants respond to mechanical stimulation such as touch with physiological changes not very different from those he observed in animal tissue. A pin prick, for example, retarded a plant's growth by 25 percent for several hours. Slashing it with a knife retarded its growth rate by the same amount for even longer.

Bose also studied the effects of stimulating plants with electricity. In one experiment, he showed that a very weak electrical impulse caused a particular part of a plant called the pulvinus to expand, whereas a strong impulse caused it to contract just as a muscle expands and contracts.

In his book *Plant Response*, which was published in 1906, Bose wrote: "As by the nerve of the animal, so also by certain conducting channels in the plant-tissue, the state of excitation is in the two cases alike, transmitted to a distance, and this conduction takes place in both by propagation of photoplasmic changes . . . the velocity of the transmission of excitation in the plant is comparable to that of its transmission in the nerves of the lower animals . . . If, then, the characteristic of nerve be to conduct excitation, it must be admitted that the plant, like the animal, is provided with a nervous system."

About a half-century later, Dr. Harold J. Burr of Yale University began to conduct his own investigations into the electrical properties of plants and animals which he termed the fields of life—L fields for short. One of the purposes behind his research was to discover the interrelationships between living organisms and their environments, terrestrial and extraterrestrial. In Dr. Burr's words, "if we could establish that living forms are affected by their electrical environment, this would show that man is an integral part of the Universe and subject to the great forces that act across space, just as the earth itself is."

We have already mentioned Dr. Burr's experiments with trees in which he showed that the rate at which a tree grows is influenced by the movements of the moon. Dr. Burr also discovered that the changes in electrical potentials that occur in trees are exactly in phase with the potentials in the earth. After he had eliminated the more common meteorological variables such as temperature, humidity, barometric pressure, etc., Burr was forced to conclude that the source of this influence produced by the moon was the change in the earth's magnetic field which the moon produced during its cycle.

Since Dr. Burr's studies, scientists have conducted innumerable experiments showing that plants that are raised near magnets will tend to grow in the direction of these magnets just as plants tend to grow in the direction of sunlight when they are kept near a window. Studies of the growth of pepper plants have shown that being raised in the presence of a magnetic field markedly accelerates the maturation of shoots and roots. In the case of wheat seedlings, there may even be as much as a 100 percent increase in the rate of their elongation. The influence of magnetic fields have also been found to produce a tenfold increase in the growth of the root of the onion plant compared with plants not exposed to the same treatment. At Michigan State University in East Lansing, Michigan, Dr. R. P. Mericle has also demonstrated accelerated growth in barley which has been exposed to magnetic fields.

These experiments thus lend credence to the observations of Dr. L. Kolisko, who was one of the first scientists to demonstrate accelerated growth in plants that were sown during particular phases of the moon. If the accelerated growth of those seedlings which were planted at the time of the full moon is some way due to the changes in the earth's magnetic field produced by the moon at this time, then there would indeed be a scientifically valid basis for that ancient bit of folk wisdom which urges farmers to plant their crops by the light of the full moon.

Scientists have also demonstrated that like plants, many primitive organisms are remarkably sensitive to alterations in their immediate magnetic field environment. Paramecia, mud snails, earthworms, and fruit flies are clearly able to distinguish between the north-south, east-west orientations of a magnetic field. Paramecia have also been found to exhibit a distinct lunar rhythm in their orientation and turning behavior. During the time of the new moon, for instance, they turn about ten degrees to the left of an imaginary zero axis passing through their bodies, whereas at the time of the full moon, they turn about ten degrees in the opposite direction, that is, to the right of an imaginary zero axis, as they move about, possibly as a result of the moon's influence on the earth's magnetic field, to which they are responsive.

It has also been suggested that the explanation for the uncanny accuracy of certain birds in crossing the oceans results from their sensitivity to the earth's magnetic field. If the flight path of these birds is examined in relation to the magnetic force field of the earth, it then appears that the accuracy of their flight pattern is achieved by maintaining a fixed orientation to the magnetic south which parallels the magnetic meridians.

In a recent issue of *Science*, Drs. Charles Walcott and Robert Green of the Department of Cellular and Comparative Biology at the State University of New York at Stony Brook, reported the results of an experimental study which clearly demonstrated the dependence of homing pigeons on magnetic fields for their unerring ability to find their way back to their homes.

Their experiment first involved training the birds to fly from the release site to their goals under both sunny and overcast conditions. Before they were released, however, the pigeons were fitted with specially devised "hats" which were constructed of coils of wire and a small battery, which together produced a small magnetic field around the pigeon's head. By simply reversing the position of the battery, the direction of the magnetic field around each bird's head could also be reversed. In addition to their magnetic hats, the pigeons were also equipped with tiny radio beacons so that their movements could always be monitored if they strayed from their designated routes.

Drs. Walcott and Green found that on sunny days, the birds flew in the right direction from their release point regardless of the position of the electrical fields around their heads. When the sun was not visible, the pigeons whose magnetic field pointed in a southerly direction also had little trouble finding home. However, when the field pointed in a northerly direction, the pigeons headed in the wrong direction.

The experiment thus showed that homing pigeons use the sun as their major cue in direction finding but that when the sun is not visible, they probably rely on the earth's magnetic field. This is even more probable in light of the fact that the strength of the earth's magnetic field is more pronounced on overcast days than on sunny days.

In the Department of Psychology at the University of Manitoba in Winnipeg, Dr. Michael Persinger has also been experimenting with the effects of exposure to magnetic fields on animals. In the course of these studies, he has found a significant increase in the locomotor activity of rats exposed to such stimulation compared to nonexposed rats.

These and many other studies from scientific laboratories across the continent clearly demonstrate that animals are sensitive to fluctuations in magnetic fields and that this sensitivity can have important effects on their behavior. Moreover, in light of these findings, it is conceivable that the increase in locomotor activity that hamsters and rats and many other animals undergo during specific phases of the moon also is connected with the moon's effect on the earth's magnetic field. In this context, it is also quite interesting to note that many people claim that they have difficulty falling or staying asleep when there is a full moon. Quite possibly, their restlessness on such nights is due to a mammalian inheritance which makes them more "nervous" during these times. This restlessness may account for the increased number of births that occur during the full moon. We can safely conclude that these births were also conceived during the full moon because the human gestation period is exactly nine lunar months, i.e., 266 days, which means that the day of the moon's cycle that an individual was born on is the same day in the moon's cycle that he was conceived on. Amusing though it may seem, we know from natural "catastrophes" such as the great blackout that occurred on the East Coast of the United States on "Black Tuesday" (November 9, 1965), that when there is nothing else for people to do, and they cannot fall asleep, they find some way of entertaining themselves. This entertainment ultimately resulted in a minor "baby boom" in that part of the country, and as we have already noted, "Black Tuesday" was not completely black—there was a full moon out that night. Thus, if the full moon keeps people awake, and also in some way acts to synchronize the female menstrual cycle so that women are in a fertile condition at such times, then this set of circumstances could readily account for the increased population on the maternity ward during the nights of the full moon.

Additional support for the moon's effect on the birth rate has also been reported by Dr. Michael Gauquelin of the Laboratoire d'Étude des Relations entre Rhythmes Cosmiques et Psychophysiologiques ("Laboratory for the Study of Relationships Between Cosmic Rhythms and

Psychophysiology") in Paris, France. According to his exhaustive studies, there is unmistakable evidence that alterations in geomagnetic activity bear a significant relationship to birth statistics, and Gauquelin hypothesizes that the moon could in some way "provoke" a disturbance in the earth's magnetic field sufficient enough to be felt by the child so that a synchronization between birth and the position of the moon occurs.

Before we go on to consider some of the other effects of the moon on human behavior, let us return to another important relationship between the moon and biological function. Recall that one of the early so-called superstitions that has now been shown to be based on fact, is that blood clotting time is affected by the cycle of the moon. This was reported several years ago by Dr. Edson J. Andrews, who discovered that the greatest extent of postoperative bleeding occurred around the time of the full moon. While not directly related to clotting time, a number of studies by Japanese scientists bear on the issue since they have shown that during periods of increased solar activity, and hence increased magnetic activity on earth, the number of leucocytes in the blood decreases. The leucocytes are the white blood cells of the blood stream and their job is to destroy any injurious substances that enter the body. Consequently, any reduction in their number could result in a lowering of the body's resistance to disease. The fact that this reduction in leucocyte count may indeed be due to increased terrestrial magnetism has been demonstrated experimentally by exposing animals in the laboratory to magnetic fields of different intensities. Whether the magnetic field fluctates naturally as a result of extraterrestrial influences, or deliberately due to experimental manipulation, the result is the same—the leucocyte count, and hence the resistance of the body, may be dangerously lowered. This may in turn be related to the increased number of deaths from cardiovascular diseases that also occur during periods of increased terrestrial magnetism.

The sensitivity of the human body to very weak electromagnetic fields similar to those normally found in nature is an area of interest that has only recently gained and held the attention of our scientists. Just a little while ago, such an idea was greeted with considerable skepticism by the scientific community, since human beings have always been exposed to a great many sources of electromagnetism, all without any apparent effect. This is no longer the consensus. As more and more information becames available, we are quickly learning that electromagnetism does have great impact not only on the health of our bodies, but on our minds as well.

In one experiment that was designed to prove the sensitivity of humans to magnetic fields, a group of subjects was led into a darkened room and was placed between two weak electromagnets. The experiment involved a test of their reaction times, and the subjects were required to press and promptly release a telegraph key as soon as they noticed the appearance of a red light positioned seven feet in front of them. It was found that their reaction time—that is, the time between the onset of the light to the time that the subject finally pressed the telegraph key—was significantly longer when the subjects performed the task in the electromagnetic field than under control conditions when the field was not activated. Apparently, the increased magnetic field in the experimental condition had slowed the transmission of nervous impulses somewhere along the pathway from the eye to the brain or the brain to the hand, or both.

While an increase in reaction time may seem like a trivial effect, consider the untold number of situations where even a delay in a fraction of a second could have disastrous results. Car accidents could increase, for example, because drivers take a second longer to react to danger, and of course, so-called pilot error may cost the lives of hundreds of people because of a split-second delay in reaction time. We know that sunspot activity affects electromagnetism on earth, but the exact timings of these solar flare-ups are still difficult to predict in advance. This is not the case with the cycle of the moon, however. Since it too affects the intensity of the earth's magnetic field, should we not take greater care in driving our cars or postpone airplane trips around such times?

Another interesting relationship between human behavior and changes in the earth's magnetic field involves the incidence of psychiatric problems. In 1963, Dr. Robert O. Becker, a surgeon at the Syracuse Veteran's Administration Hospital, reported the results of a study he conducted in conjunction with two other physicians, in which he compared the number of admissions to seven central psychiatric hospitals in New York State with variations in the earth's magnetic field intensity. The unmistakable correlation prompted Dr. Becker to conclude in a statement he gave to *Newsweek* magazine (May 13, 1963) that even minute changes in the strength of the earth's magnetic field can affect the human nervous system. When magnetic disturbances increase, nervous activity in the brain increases, and in some people, these result in an outbreak of mental illness. When magnetic disturbances decrease, on the other hand, the number of patients seeking admittance or being brought to the mental hospital forcibly also decreases. "Attention is thus invited," writes Dr. Becker and his colleagues, "to a hitherto neglected dimension in the complexity of psychopathology specifically, and perhaps generally in all human behavior."

Do these observations also account for the increased number of admissions to psychiatric hospitals during the full moon? Since the moon also produces an intensity in geomagnetism when it is full, it is not inconceivable that the increased agitation of the mentally ill is due to the increased electrical brain activity that they experience when the earth's magnetic field increases.

Mental illnesses may also take forms other than admis
sion to mental hospitals. Instead of seeking out help
mentally ill individuals may become violent toward other
or to themselves. We have already noted that there i
an increase in the suicide rate during the period of th
full moon. This same increase also occurs during period
of heightened solar activity. The peculiar sensitivity o
certain human beings to magnetic fields has also bee
cited by Dr. Yves Rocard, Director of the Physic
Laboratory at the University of Paris, as the basis fo
the ancient practice of "dowsing"—searching for wate
by means of a divining rod. Dr. Rocard acknowledge
that the ability of dowsers to find water is generally re
garded as nothing short of superstition, but nonethe
less, he contends that in many cases, when certai
geophysical conditions are present, some kind of stimulu
often causes the hands of the dowser to move the divining
rod up or downward independently of his will. While the
direct effects of water on the movement of the divining
rod is not admitted, Dr. Rocard does point out that wate
is in fact very frequently found at the place where thi
bizarre movement of the divining rod occurs. In examining
this phenomenon, Dr. Rocard found that one of the im
portant factors influencing the dowser may be the earth'
magnetic field, since in the hands of an expert, the move
ment of the divining rod often occurs in regions where
the earth's magnetic field is not completely uniform. The
greater the anomaly in the geomagnetic pattern, the
greater the "signal" and "no supplementary muscula
contraction succeeds in restraining the rod."

The reason that water is often found by this sensitivity
to magnetic fields, Dr. Rocard explains, is that whe
water filters through porous material, or is present i
permeable layers near beds of clay, it produces a weak
electrical current like that of a concentration battery
Should the medium of the earth in the vicinity be suffi
ciently conducting, the current in the soil would then ac

like a small electromagnet, producing the magnetic anomaly capable of being sensed by the dowser. Although the actions of a magnetic field are not typically felt by humans, it has been demontrated that under conditions of increased sensitivity such as following hypnosis or mescaline intoxication, otherwise unresponsive individuals can be made sensitive to this type of stimulation. Apparently in the case of the expert dowser, this sensitivity to magnetic fields is already present. The plausibility of this explanation is supported by the fact that expert dowsers are able to detect the presence of experimentally produced electromagnetic fields in the laboratory where such fields may be turned on or off without the dowser's knowledge.

One such experiment of this type was conducted by the Dutch scientist Dr. S. W. Tromp. Under his careful supervision, artificial magnetic fields were set up in particular areas through which a number of dowsers were required to walk. The dowsers were also required to wear special equipment which enabled Tromp to monitor their electrocardiograms and to take measurements of the intensities of the magnetic field at all times. Tromp found it was indeed true that dowsers were capable of detecting very minute changes in magnetic fields on the order of one millioersted, which is far lower than the strength of the earth's magnetic field. Since this intensity of magnetic flux is far too small to have affected a dowser's rod on its own, Tromp suggested that the minute change in the magnetic field produced by underground water causes the muscles of the dowser's arm to contract very slightly and this contraction results in the movement of the divining rod.

"Whatever it is," writes Professor Rocard, "the curious phenomenon of the dowser's reflex, inasmuch as it is caused by a small magnetic variation, obliges us to consider wholly new possibilities for magnetic reaction on living matter."

These experiments with plants, with animals, and above all with human beings thus make it abundantly clear that living organisms are responsive to magnetic changes emanating from our earth. In many cases such changes in the earth's magnetic field are produced by the moon, and it is no wonder, then, that the moon exerts such a potentially important influence over our behavior. It has done so in the past, it is doing so in the present, and it will surely continue to do so in the future. As we grow to understand this influence and appreciate its impact on all the living organisms that inhabit our earth, it is possible that someday we may be able to utilize that influence to the betterment of our lives beyond merely enjoying the shimmering splendor of our only natural satellite as it circles our globe on its monthly cycle through the heavens.

Bibliography

TIME, BLOOD, AND THE MOON

Andrews, E. J. "Moon Talk. The Cyclic Periodicity of Postoperative Hemorrhage," *Journal of the Florida State Medical Association*, 1961, *46*, 1362-1366

Frazer, J. G. *The Golden Bough*. Macmillan & Co., London, 1900.

Harley, T. *Moon Lore*. Swan, Sonnenscheim, LaBus and Lowry, London, 1885.

La Martinière. Quoted by Harley.

Watson, L. *Supernature*. Anchor Press, New York, 1973.

BIOLOGISTS DISCOVER THE MOON

Adderley, E. E., and Bowen, E. G. "Lunar Component in Precipitation Data," *Science*, 1962, *137*, 749-750.

Bradley, D. A., Woodbury, M. A., and Brier, G. W. "Lunar Synodical Period and Widespread Precipitation," *Science*, 1962, *137*, 748-749.

Brown, F. A. "Persistent Activity Rhythms in the Oyster," *American Journal of Physiology*, 1954, *178*, 510-514.

Brown, F. A. "Propensity for Lunar Periodicity in Hamsters and Its Significance for Biological Clock Theories," *Proceedings of the Society for Experimental Biology and Medicine*, 1965, *120*, 792-797.

Brown, F. A., and Park, Y. H. "Synodic Monthly Modulation

of the Diurnal Rhythm of Hamsters," *Proceedings of th* *Society for Experimental Biology and Medicine,* 1967, *12:* 712-713.

Brown, F. A., Webb, H. M., and Bennett, M. K. "Proof for a Endogenous Component in Persistent Solar and Lunar Rhyth micity in Organisms," *Proceedings of the National Acad emy of Sciences,* 1955, *41,* 93-100.

Brown, F. A., Shriner, J., and Ralph, C. L. "Solar and Luna Rhythmicity in the Rat in Constant Conditions and th Mechanism of Physiological Time Measurement," *America Journal of Physiology,* 1956, *184,* 491-496.

Fingerman, M. "Lunar Rhythmicity in Marine Organisms, *American Naturalist,* 1957, *91,* 167-178.

Tchijevsky, A. L. "Physical Factors of the Historical Process, *Cycles,* 1971, *22,* 11-21.

Terracini, E. D., and Brown, F. A. "Periodism in Mouse 'Spor taneous' Activity Synchronized with Major Geophysica Cycles," *Physiological Zoology,* 1962, *35,* 27-37.

4. SEX AND THE MOON

Aristotle. *On The Nature of Animals.*

Aristotle. *On The Generation of Animals.*

Burrows, W. "Periodic Spawning of 'Palolo' Worms in Pacifi Waters," *Nature,* 1945, *155,* 47-48.

Clark, L. B. "Factors in the Lunar Cycle Which May Contro Reproduction in the Atlantic Palolo," *Biological Bulletin o the Marine Biology Laboratory,* 1941, *81,* 278.

Cowgill, Y. M., Bishop, A., Andrew R. J., and Hutchinson, G. E "An Apparent Lunar Periodicity in the Sexual Cycle o Certain Prosimians," *Proceedings of the Natural Academy o Sciences,* 1962, *48,* 232-241.

Crawshay, L. R. "Possible Bearing of a Luminous Syllid on th Question of the Landfall of Columbus," *Nature,* 1935, *13C* 559-560.

Darwin, C. *The Descent of Man.* London, 1871.

Ellis, H. *Studies in the Psychology of Sex.* Random House, New York, 1942.

Fox, H. M. "Periodicity in Reproduction," *Proceedings of th Royal Society of London,* 1923, *95,* 523-550.

Fox, H. M. *Selene, or Sex and the Moon.* Kegan Paul, Trench and Teubner, London, 1928.

Fox, H. M. "Lunar Periodicity of Reproduction," *Nature,* 1932 *130,* 23.

Harrison, J. L. "Moonlight and Pregnancy of Malayan Forest Rats," *Nature*, 1952, *170*, 73.

Harrison, J. L. "Breeding Rhythms of Rodents," *Bulletin of the Raffles Museum*, 1952, *24*, 109-131.

Harrison, J. L. "The Moonlight Effect on Rat Breeding," *Bulletin of the Raffles Museum*, 1954, *25*, 166-170.

Hartland-Rowe, R. "The Biology of a Tropical May Fly, *Povilla adresta,* with Special Reference to the Lunar Rhythm of Emergence," *Revue Zoologie et Botanie d'Africa*, 1958, *58*, 185-186.

Hauenschild, C. "Neue Experimentelle untersuchangen zum Problem du Lunar Periodizität," *Naturwissenschaften*, 1956, *43*, 361-369.

Huntsman, A. G. "*Odontosyllis* at Permuda and Lunar Periodicity," *Journal of the Fisheries Research Board of Canada*, 1948, *1*, 363-369.

Korriga, P. "Lunar Periodicity," *Memoirs of the Geological Society*, 1957, *1*, 917-934.

Mason, J. "A Possible Lunar Periodicity in the Breeding of the Scallop *Pecten maximus* (L)," *Annals of the Magazine of Natural History*, 1958, *1*, 601-602.

McDowell, R. M. "Lunar Rhythms in Aquatic Animals," *Tuatara*, 1969, *17*, 133-144.

Morison, S. E. *Christopher Columbus, Mariner.* Little, Brown and Co., Boston, 1955.

Ramanathan, O. "Light and Sexual Periodicity in Indian Buffaloes," *Nature*, 1952, *130*, 169-170.

Ray, H., and Chakraverty, M. "Lunar Periodicity in the Conjugation of *Conchophthirius lamellidens* Ghosh," *Nature*, 1934, *134*, 663-664.

Walker, B. W. "A Guide to the Grunion," *California Fish and Game*, 1952, *38*, 409-420.

5. THE MOON'S INFLUENCE ON WOMEN

Aelian. *On Animals.*

Aristotle. *On the Generation of Animals.*

Arrhenius, S. "Die Einwirkung Einflusse auf Physiologische Verhaltnisse," *Skandinavishe Archiv fur Physiologie*, 1898, *8*, 367-416.

Bacon, F. *Sylvia Sylvarum.*

Cicero. *On the Nature of Things.*

Dewan, E. M. "On the Possibility of a Perfect Rhythm Method of Birth Control by Periodic Light Stimulation," *American*

Journal of Obstetrics and Gynecology, 1967, *98*, 656-659.

Foissac, P. "Influence of Lunar Phases on Physical Moral Man," *St. Louis Medical and Surgical Journal*, 1885, *13*, 502-517.

Frazer, J. G. *The Golden Bough*. Macmillan & Co., London, 1900.

Gunn, D. L., and Jenkins, P. M. "Lunar Periodicity in Homo Sapiens," *Nature*, 1937, *139*, 84.

Guthmann, H., and Oswald, D. "Menstruation und Mond," *Manschrift fur Geburtsch und Gynakologie*, 1936, *103*, 232-235.

Kaiser, I. H., and Halberg, F. "Circadian Periodic Aspects of Birth," *Annals of the New York Academy of Sciences*, 1962, *98*, 1056-1058.

Malek, J., Gleich, J., and Maly, V. "Characteristics of the Daily Rhythm of Menstruation and Labor," *Annals of the New York Academy of Sciences*, 1962, *98*, 1042-1055.

6. THE MOON AND THE MATERNITY WARD

Andrews, E. J. "Moon Talk," *Journal of the Florida State Medical Association*, 1961, *46*, 1362-1366.

Anonymous. "The Moon and Medicine," *Clinicial Excerpts*, 1940, *14*, 5-11.

Beamer-Maxwell, E., and Hendrick, H. F. M. Quoted by Ravitz.

Charles, E. "The Hour of Birth, A Study of Distribution of Times of Onset Labor and of Delivery throughout the 24-hour Period," *British Journal of Preventive Social Medicine*, 1953, *7*, 43-59.

Menaker, W., and Menaker, A. "Lunar Periodicity in Human Reproduction," *American Journal of Obstetrics and Gynecology*, 1959, *77*, 905-913.

Menaker, W. "Lunar Periodicity with Reference to Live Births," *American Journal of Obstetrics and Gynecology*, 1967, *98*, 1002-1004.

Oberndorf, C. P. "Sexual Periodicity in the Male," *Medical Record*, 1913, *84*, 18-20.

Osley, M., Summerville, D., and Borst, L. B. "Natality and the Moon," *American Journal of Obstetrics and Gynecology*, 1973, *117*, 413-415.

Palmer, J. D. "The Many Clocks of Man," *Cycles*, 1971, *4*, 36-41.

Persinger, M. A. "Prenatal Exposure to an ELF Rotating Magnetic Field, Ambulatory Behavior, and Lunar Distance at Birth: A Correlation," *Psychological Reports*, 1971, *28*, 435-438.

Points, T. C. "Twenty-four Hours in a Day," *Obstetrics et Gynecologie,* 1956, *2,* 245-248.

Ravitz, L. J. "Electrodynamic Field Theory in Psychiatry," *Southern Medical Journal,* 1953, *46,* 650-660.

Rippmann, E. T. "The Moon and the Birth Rate," *American Journal of Obstetrics and Gynecology,* 1957, *74,* 148-150.

Schnurhman, A. G. "The Effect of the Moon on Childbirth," *Virginia Medical Monthly,* 1949, *76,* 78.

Shettles, L. B. "Variations in Onset Labor and Rupture of Membranes," *American Journal of Obstetrics and Gynecology,* 1960, *79,* 177-179.

Simpson, A. S. "Are More Babies Born at Night?" *British Medical Journal,* 1952, *2,* 832-834.

7. THE MOON AND THE GROWTH OF PLANTS

Bacon, F. *Sylvia Sylvarum.*

Beeson, C. F. C. "Forestry, Horticulture and the Moon," *Forestry Abstracts,* 1946, *8,* 191-198.

Berger, F. D. *Current Superstitions Collected from the Oral Traditions of English Speaking Folk.* Houghton Mifflin & Co., New York, 1896.

Brown, F. A. "Endogenous Biorhythmicity Reviewed with New Evidence," *Scientia,* 1962, *103,* 1-6.

Brown, F. A., and Chow, C. S. "Lunar-correlated Variations in Water Uptake by Bean Seeds," *Biological Bulletin,* 1973, *145,* 265-278.

Burr, H. S. "Moon-Madness," *Yale Journal of Biology and Medicine,* 1943, *16,* 249-256.

De La Quintinye. *Instructions pour les Jardains, Fruiters et Potagers, avec un tracte des Oranges survi quelques Instructions sur l'Agriculture.* Paris, 1690.

Du Monceau, J. *De l'exploration des bois.* Paris, 1764.

Frazier, J. G. *The Golden Bough.* Macmillan & Co., London, 1900.

Gates, F. C. "Influence of Moonlight on the Movement of Leguminous Leaflets," *Ecology,* 1923, *4,* 37-39.

Grew, N. *The Anatomy of Plants.* London, 1682.

Kittredge G. L. *The Old Farmer and His Almanac.* Harvard University Press, Cambridge, 1924.

Kolisko, L. *The Moon and the Growth of Plants.* Anthroposophical Agricultural Foundation, Brag-on-Thames, 1936.

Lestz, G. S. *Moon Lore.* John Baer's Sons, Lancaster, Pa., no date.

Mather, M. "The Effect of Temperature and the Moon on Seed-
     ling Growth," *Journal of the Royal Horticulture Society*,
     1942, *67*, 264-270.
Mather, K., and Newell, J. "Seed Germination and the Moon,"
     Journal of the Royal Horticulture Society, 1941, *66*, 358-
     366.
Pliny. *Natural History*.
Plutarch. Quoted by Tavenner.
Semmens, E. S. "Effect of Moonlight on the Germination of
     Seeds," *Nature*, 1923, *111*, 49.
Tavenner, E. "The Roman Farmer and the Moon," *Transactions
     and Proceedings of the American Philological Association*,
     1918, *49*, 67-82.
Tavenner, E. "Roman Moon Lore," *Washington University
     Studies*, 1920, *8*, 39-59.

8. THE "FALLING SICKNESS"

Arataeus. *Works*. London, 1856.
Hildegard of Bigen. Quoted by Thorndike.
Hunter, J. *Works*. Longman Rees & Co., London, 1835.
Kepler, J. *Works* (I. 608-611).
Laycock, T. "On Lunar Influence," *Lancet*, 1842, *2*, 440-444.
Maimonides, M. *A Guide for the Perplexed*.
Mead, R. *A Treatise Concerning the Influence of the Sun and
     Moon upon Human Bodies and the Diseases Thereby Pro-
     duced*. London, 1746.
Moreau, J. *De l'Etiologie de l'Epilepsie*. Memoirs de l'Academie
     de Medicine, Paris, 1854.
Oribasius. Quoted by Thorndike.
Petersen, W. *The Patient and the Weather*. C. C. Thomas, Spring-
     field, Ill., 1947.
Ptolemy. *Tetrabiblos*.
Romberg, M. H. *A Manual of the Nervous Diseases of Man*.
     Sydenham Society, London, 1853.
Sieveking, E. H. *On Epilepsy and Epileptiform Seizures*. John
     Churchill, London, 1858.
Stahl, W. "Moon Madness," *Annals of Medical History*, 1937, *9*,
     248-263.
Tempkin, O. *The Falling Sickness*. John Hopkins Press, Balti-
     more, 1971.
Thorndike, L. *History of Magic and Experimental Science*. Mac-
     millan & Co., New York, 1923.

Winslow, F. B. *Light: Its Influence on Life and Health.* Long-man's Green, London, 1867.

9. MOON MADNESS

The Historical Perspective

Anonymous. "The Moon and Medicine," *Clinical Excerpts*, 1940, *14*, 5-11.

Boyle, R. *Experimenta et Observationes Physical.*

Briffault, R. *The Mothers.* Macmillan & Co., New York, 1927.

Daquin, M. *Philosophie de la Folie.* Paris, 1791.

Esquirol, E. *Mental Maladies.* Lea and Blanchard, Philadelphia, 1845.

Griesinger, W. *Mental Pathology and Therapeutics.* New Sydenham Co., London, 1867.

Hale, M. *History of the Pleas of the Crown.* Columbia University Press, New York, 1949.

Harley, T. *Moon Lore.* Swan, Sonnenscheim, LaBus and Lowry, London, 1885.

Haslam, J. *Observations on Madness and Melancholy.* London, 1809.

Hunter, J. *Works.* Longman Rees & Co., London, 1835.

King, H. D. "Medicine and the Moon," *Medical Record*, 1917, *94*.

Paracelsus. *Diseases That Deprive Man of Health and Reason.*

Rush, B. *Medical Inquiries and Observations upon Diseases of the Mind.* Gregg and Co., Philadelphia, 1835.

Sarton, G. "Lunar Influences on Living Things," *Isis*, 1939, *30*, 498-507.

Tuke, D. H. *Chapters in the History of the Insane.* Kegan Paul, Trench and Co., London, 1882.

Ward, E. H. P. "The Moon and Insanity," *Medical Record*, 1919, *96*, 318-320.

Modern Views

Bauer, S. F., and Hornick, E. J. "Lunar Effects on Mental Illness," *American Journal of Psychiatry*, 1968, *125*, 696-697.

Burr, H. S., and Northrop, F. S. C. "Evidence for the Existence of an Electrodynamic Field in Living Organisms," *Proceedings of the National Academy of Sciences*, 1939, *25*, 284-288.

Deutsch, A. *The Mentally Ill in America.* Columbia University Press, New York, 1949.

Kelley, D. "Mania and the Moon," *Psychoanalytical Review,* 1942, *29,* 406-426.

Lilienfeld, D. M. "Lunar Effect on Mental Illness," *American Journal of Psychiatry,* 1969, *125,* 1454.

Oliven, J. F. "Moonlight and Nervous Disorders," *American Journal of Psychiatry,* 1942, *99,* 579-584.

Osborn, R. D. "The Moon and the Mental Hospital: An Investigation of the Area of Folklore," *Journal of Psychiatric Nursing,* 1962, *6,* 88-93.

Pokorny, A. D. "Moon Phases and Mental Hospital Admissions," *Journal of Psychiatric Nursing,* 1962, *6,* 325-327.

Ravitz, L. J. "Electrodynamic Field Theory in Psychiatry," *Southern Medical Journal,* 1953, *46,* 650-660.

Ravitz, L. J. "Comparative Clinical and Electrocyclic Observations on Twin Brothers," *Journal of Nervous and Mental Diseases,* 1955, *121,* 72-87.

Sarton, G. "Lunar Influence on Living Things," *Isis,* 1939, *30,* 495-507.

Shapiro, J. L., Streiner, D. L., and Gray, A. L. "The Moon and Mental Illness," *Perceptual Motor Skills,* 1970, *30,* 827-830.

Spurzheim, J. C. *Observations on the Deranged Manifestations of the Mind on Insanity.* March Capen and Lyon Co., Boston, 1883.

Stahl, W. H. "Moon Madness," *Annals of Medical History,* 1937, *9,* 248-263.

Trapp, C. E. "Lunacy and the Moon," *American Journal of Psychiatry,* 1937, *94,* 334-339.

White, W. A. "Moon Myth in Medicine," *Psychoanalytical Review,* 1914, *1,* 241-251.

10. MURDER BY MOONLIGHT

Lieber, A. L., and Sherin, C. R. "Homicides and the Lunar Cycle," *American Journal of Psychiatry,* 1972, *129,* 69-74.

Pokorny, A. D. "Moon Phases, Suicide and Homicide," *American Journal of Psychiatry,* 1964, *121,* 66-67.

Timmins, C. *Planting by the Moon.* Aries Press, Chicago, 1939.

11. SUICIDE

Lester, D., Brockopp, G. W., and Priebe, K. "Association Between a Full Moon and Completed Suicide," *Psychological Reports*, 1969, *25*, 598.

Ossenkopp, K. P., and Ossenkopp, M. D. "Self-Inflicted Injuries and the Lunar Cycle," *Journal of Interdisciplinary Cycle Research*, 1973, *4*, 337-348.

Petersen, W. *The Patient and the Weather*. C. C. Thomas, Springfield, Ill., 1949.

Pokorny, A. D. "Moon Phases, Suicide and Homicide," *American Journal of Psychiatry*, 1964, *121*, 66-67.

Taylor, L. J., and Diespecker, D. D. "Moon Phases and Suicide Attempts in Australia," *Psychological Reports*, 1972, *31*, 112.

12. LYCANTHROPY (THE WEREWOLF SYNDROME)

Baring-Gould, S. *The Book of Were-wolves*. Smith, Elder and Co., London, 1868.

McDaniel, W. B. "The Moon, Werewolves and Medicine," *Transactions of Studies of the College of Physicians of Philadelphia*, 1950, 18, 113-122.

Seabrook, W. *Witchcraft, Its Power in the World Today*.

Summers, M. *The Werewolf*. Citadel Press, Secaucus, N. J., 1973.

13. LUNAMBULISM

Sadger, J. *Sleep Walking and Moon Walking*. Nervous and Mental Disease Monographs, New York, 1920.

14. ELECTRICITY AND MAGNETISM

King, J. W. "Weather and the Earth's Magnetic Field," *Nature*, 1974, *247*, 131-134.

Mulder, J. B. "Animal Behavior and Electromagnetic Energy Waves," *Laboratory Animal Science*, 1971, *21*, 389-393.

Ott, J. N. "Some Responses of Plants and Animals to Variations in Wave Lengths of Light Energy," *Annals of the New York Academy of Sciences*, 1964, *117*, 624-635.

Spaulding, J. F., Archuleta, R. F., and Holland, L. M. "Influence of the Visible Colour Spectrum on Activity in Mice," *Laboratory Animal Care*, 1969, *19*, 50-54.

15. THE SCIENTIFIC BASIS FOR THE MOON'S EFFECTS ON LIVING ORGANISMS

Audus, L. "Magnetropism: A New Plant-Growth Response,"
    Nature, 1960, *185*, 132-133.

Barnothy, J. "Growth Rate of Mice in Static Magnetic Fields,"
    Nature, 1963, *200*, 86.

Barnothy, M. "Development of Young Mice," in *Biological
    Effects of Magnetic Fields*, ed. Barnothy, M. Plenum Press,
    New York, 1964.

Barnwell, F., and Brown, F. "Responses of Planarians and
    Snails," in *Biological Effects of Magnetic Fields*, ed. Barno-
    thy, M. Plenum Press, New York, 1964.

Gauquelin, M. "Genetic Sensitivity to External Factors during
    the Daily Cycle of Deliveries," *Journal of Interdisciplinary
    Cycle Research*, 1971, *2*, 227-232.

Gordon, D. "Sensitivity of the Homing Pigeon to the Magnetic
    Field of the Earth," *Science*, 1948, *108*, 710-711.

Mericle, R. "Plant Growth Response," in *Biological Effects of
    Magnetic Fields*, ed. Barnothy, M. Plenum Press, New
    York, 1964.

Presman, A. S. *Electromagnetic Fields and Life*. Plenum Press,
    New York, 1970.

Tromp, S. W. *Medical Biometeorology*. Elsvier Pub. Co., New
    York, 1963.

Walcott, C., and Green, R. P. "Orientation of Homing Pigeons
    Altered by a Change in the Direction of an Applied Mag-
    netic Field," *Science*, 1974, *184*, 180-182.